Praise for the Dating Goddess

The *Adventures in Delicious Dating After 40* series of books is based on the blog Adventures in Delicious Dating After 40 at www.DatingGoddess.com. Here are comments from readers.

- "Adventures in Delicious Dating After 40 is a wonderful composite of both the mechanics of post-40 online dating and what the practice of honoring one's self actually looks like. How marvelous your writing is to read. I spent about 2 hours reading and was riveted the whole time." —Maggie Hanna

- "At last, a dating writer who addresses requirements. You are SO right on! I'm thrilled to have found you!" —Rachel Sarah, author, *Single Mom Seeking*

- "Powerfully heartfelt and honest writing. You are inspiring." —Kare Anderson, Emmy Award winning writer

"I just love your writing. It is very fresh and gives the reader something to think about." —Kelly Lantz, President & Manager, 55-Alive.com

"Dating Goddess, you are like a, a, a, well, a goddess to me. You've helped guide me successfully through my re-entry into the dating world after 14 years. I'm an eager student and fast study, and do get myself into situations that others don't know how to deal with — such as 3 dates in one day —— so thankfully you are there! You're the greatest, thanks for all you do for us!" —Jae G.

"I find your point of view much more interesting than other dating writers. Thanks for always reminding me to enjoy dating life no matter what it throws at you." —Sandy

"I love Adventures in Delicious Dating After 40. I really do like your honest and authentic voice — it's refreshing." —Wendy S.

"Adventures in Delicious Dating After 40 is really fun to read. Thanks for sharing your thoughts and letting us divorced single women know that we are not alone. There's a lot here that I identify with, although I'm not as brave as you are about dating lots of guys. So far. Love your blog — the first blog I've ever read consistently." —Elizabeth

"Thanks for a wonderful blog. You're doing a great job of saying what's in my mind. There's rarely a day I miss when it comes to checking in on your wisdom." —Paulette Ensign

Moving
On
Gracefully

Break Up
Without Heartache

by **Dating Goddess**

Moving On Gracefully: Break Up Without Heartache

Second Edition

Cover design by Dave Innis, www.innisanimation.com

Book design by JustYourType.biz

Printed in the United States of America.

ISBN   Print: 978-1-930039-92-6

eBook: 978-1-930039-21-6

How to order:

The *Adventures in Delicious Daing After 40* books may be ordered directly from www.DatingGoddess.com.

Quantity discounts are also available. Visit us online for updates and additional articles.

The Adventures in Delicious Dating After 40 books are dedicated to my ex-husband since he unexpectedly released me to explore the untethered life of a single woman. I then had the freedom for the experiences, lessons and insights shared in these pages.

Books by Dating Goddess

❤ *Date or Wait: Are You Ready for Mr. Great?*

❤ *Assessing Your Assets: Why You're A Great Catch*

❤ *In Search of King Charming: Who Do I Want to Share My Throne?*

❤ *Embracing Midlife Men: Insights Into Curious Behaviors*

❤ *Dipping Your Toe in the Dating Pool: Dive In Without Belly Flopping*

❤ *Winning at the Online Dating Game: Stack the Deck in Your Favor*

❤ *Check Him Out Before Going Out: Avoiding Dud Dates*

❤ *First-Rate First Dates: Increasing the Chances of a Second Date*

❤ *Real Deal or Faux Beau: Should You Keep Seeing Him?*

❤ *Multidating Responsibly: Play the Field Without Being A Player*

❤ *Moving On Gracefully: Break Up Without Heartache*

❤ *From Fear to Frolic: Get Naked Without Getting Embarrassed*

❤ *Ironing Out Dating Wrinkles: Work Through Challenges Without Getting Steamed*

Contents

ix

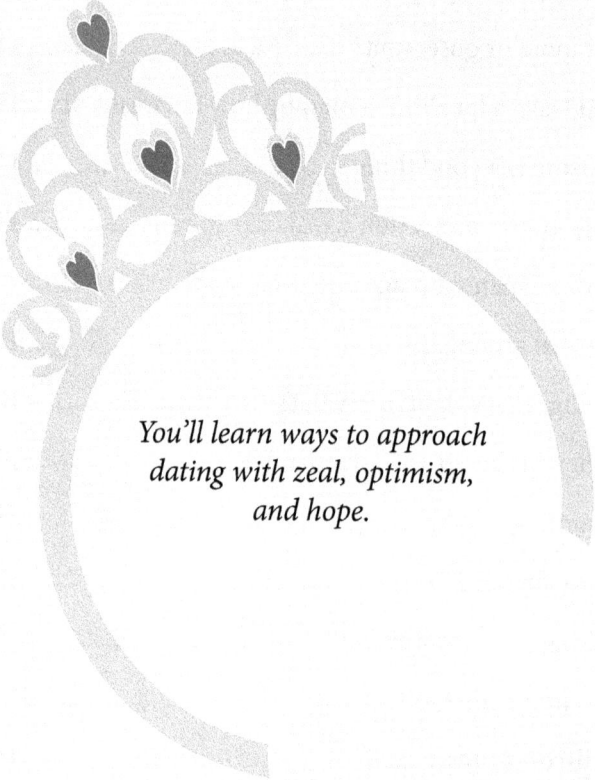

You'll learn ways to approach dating with zeal, optimism, and hope.

Introduction

This book is designed for anyone who is interested in stories, advice, and lessons from the midlife dating front. If you are over 40 and haven't dated in a while — or even if you have — you'll learn ways to approach dating with zeal, optimism, and hope. Even if you've had more than your share of negative experiences, I'll share how to glean lessons from those adventures, rather than just declaring that "all men are jerks" or "men are just looking for sex."

While most of the perspective is from a woman to women, men's comments, experiences, and lessons have been integrated as appropriate.

This book began as daily entries into my blog, Adventures in Delicious Dating After 40, which has been featured in the *Wall Street Journal* as well as on radio and TV. I wrote about my epiphanies from my and my friends' dating life. The best postings were culled to make this and subsequent books.

This book focuses on surviving a breakup, whether you initiate it or not. Either way, it's never easy to break up if you have developed any fondness toward the other.

This book consists of three types of perspectives:

💜 **Lessons:** These are specific experiences I thought would be useful to you. A few lines from my experience illustrate the points.

💜 **Insights:** These usually start with an experience I've encountered, then the insights that experience spawned. It is usually comprised of around half story and half insight.

💜 **Stories:** These are examples of situations I've experienced — or was currently experiencing when I wrote that piece — that I thought would be entertaining. Or I thought the story would help you see what kind of things happen in the midlife dating world so you'd know what has happened to others.

Because these writings were real time, as they occured, they are often set in the present tense. But they are not chronological. So a reference to "my current beau" may now be many sweethearts ago. I hope this isn't confusing.

I'd love ot hear your stories and questions. Please email them to me at Goddess@DatingGoddess.com. They may make it into the blog or my next book!

Who is the Dating Goddess?

I am a middle-aged, white, professional woman. My husband of nearly 20 years left me in April 2003 when I was 47, 11 days shy of 48. After giving my heart time to heal from the surprise divorce sprung by the man I thought was my soulmate, I started dating 18 months later. Generally, I have had a great time meeting interesting men, some of whom became romantic beaus, some became treasured friends, and some I never heard from again.

I am not a well-preserved, gorgeous, marathon-running middle-aged women

In the beginning, I had dates with single male colleagues, but I quickly found Internet dating was the way to explore the most "inventory" and qualify men who I thought might be a good match.

I am not one of those well-preserved, gorgeous,

marathon-running middle-aged women. I have been told I am attractive, but I am overweight and not a gym rat. So while I am active, I do not match the description 90% of men's profiles say they want: slender, athletic, toned, fit. I have some wrinkles — what one sweet suitor mistakenly called dimples. I have what Bridget Jones called "wobbly bits," as most non-surgically enhanced middle-aged women do. My genes — and a lifetime addiction to chocolate — have made their mark. Yet I've met and dated some wonderful men, so even if you're not a lingerie model, you can find guys who will think you're attractive, perhaps even hot!

In my professional life, I am a bestselling author of workplace effectiveness books, professional speaker and management consultant. I've appeared on Oprah, 60 Minutes, and National Public Radio and in the *Wall Street Journal* and *USA Today*.

This book is intended to not only be useful to others and cathartic for me, but is also the genesis of a new topic for fun, thought-provoking speeches. I'm calling myself a dating philosopher and giving date-a-vational speeches! Let me know if you know a group who would like an entertaining after-lunch speech on how lessons learned from dating have implications in business and personal relationships and well as life philosophies.

How did I come by the Dating Goddess moniker? After a few months of dating dozens of men — one week yielded 7 dates with 6 guys in 5 days — my friends dubbed me this name. I liked it, so it stuck.

I'm purposefully not sharing my picture as I don't want you to think either, "How did she get any dates at all?" or the opposite, "Of course she found it easy to get 112 men to ask her out." I am not hideous (usually) nor am I stunning (without professional hair, makeup and Photoshop!). Some men find me attractive, some don't.

I continue to search for my "one," but I have learned a lot along the way, and my single and not-single friends have loudly encouraged me to share my experiences and lessons in the hopes of helping others navigate the adventure of dating with more success. And to have a delicious time doing it!

xx

*Make sure to download your free
eBook, "Dating Advice from XX
Top Relationship Experts" at www.
DatingGoddess.com/freebie*

How to say "thanks but no thanks" to online winks, flirts and teases

W hen someone is not a member of a dating site — or they are lazy — they float a trial balloon by clicking on "Wink" (depending on the site, these are also called flirts, teases or ice breakers).

I am convinced some men do a rudimentary search by criteria such as "breathing" and "lives on the planet Earth" and then wink at every woman who comes up. I say this because I get winks from men who are not just outside my region, but are not in the same state or country. This is like fishing with a net, versus the more skill-based fly fishing — they are just seeing who will respond to their broad contacts.

I've had winks from men 30 years younger, 20 years older, 5 inches shorter, lived on other continents, and who are far off my other criteria. On one level, I admire their boldness. On another level, I want to say, "Do you really think the Goddess would consider going out with a 27-year-old movie usher who lives with his parents and rides his bike to work because he doesn't have a car?"

So what to do? Do you just ignore them? If you get a lot of winks — say 5 or more a day —then you have to. But I like to respond to every contact, no matter how lame or mismatched. So I have a macro saved with a polite "no thanks." By typing 3 letters I get the following:

Thanks for your wink.

I'm sure you are a nice guy. I appreciate your interest in me; however, I don't think we'd be a good match.

Good luck in your search. I wish you the best!

I've even been thanked for how I say no! It seems so many people don't respond to any contact — whether wink or email — that any response is considered polite and classy.

Create your own polite message so you can just cut and paste.

I like to respond to every contact, no matter how mismatched

Hello — goodbye: How to say no thanks after meeting

One of the hardest parts of dating is telling your date that it isn't a match so you don't encourage him to pursue you.

It is easiest to do in an email. I recommend this method if you've only met once. Start with thanking him for coffee, lunch, whatever. Comment on some of his positive characteristics. Then tell him it's not a match:

"Thank you for treating for coffee and our interesting discussion. You certainly know a lot about politics.

"You are an intelligent, warm, fun gentleman. However, I don't feel we are a match. The right woman will snap you up soon!"

Harder is on the phone. I've had to do this when a guy calls to set up a second date. It is uncomfortable, but you need to be gentle yet honest — up to a point. Recently, after the guy asked when he could see me again, I said, "I appreciate your interest in me, but we're not a match. You are a nice, fun guy, but I don't feel we have enough in common to continue seeing each other. And it wouldn't be fair to you to accept another date knowing that I don't feel the spark I know needs to be there to develop a relationship."

He said he was disappointed, but he understood. He said, "So I've gained a new friend."

"Exactly," I replied.

> It wouldn't be fair to you to accept another date

The hardest way to communicate your lack of interest is in person. I've not done this often. It is definitely uncomfortable. The other day at the end of an initial lunch, the man said, "So what happens next?" He wouldn't have said this unless he was interested in a second date.

"We need to decide if we both want to spend more time together," I replied.

"It's up to the woman," he said, "so what do you want to have happen next?"

I squirmed. "Since you are new to online dating, I suggest you date some more women," was the best I could muster. I just couldn't be blunt and say, "I don't really want to go out again." While many men appreciate honesty, they also have fragile egos.

I followed up with a thank you email wishing him well in his dating adventures. That made it clear.

You don't need to go into a review of all the things he said or did that were a turn off: how he used his finger for a pusher on his plate rather than a knife, interrupted you a lot, rarely asked anything about you, picked up his lamb chops with his fingers to eat them, or showed up at the nice restaurant in sweats. No, most men don't want to know that kind of detail. And what may have been annoying to you may not be to the next woman.

Strive to be kind, gentle, and to allow him to keep his dignity. I always appreciate it when a guy does that to me.

DatingGoddess.com

6

Releasing back into the dating pool

oesn't this phrase sound benign? Refreshing even? Can you imagine a perfect-temperature, clear, tranquil pool, inviting you to dip your toes or immerse yourself totally in the rejuvenating water? Do you see yourself floating on the pristine pond as the gentle current rocks you into complete relaxation?

If only releasing someone — or being released — back into the dating pool was so calm. In fact, it is usually the opposite, full of stress, teeth gnashing, crying, yelling or drama. Often there are hurt feelings on one or both sides. Whether you are the releaser or the released, the relationship-liberating conversation typically entails tension, even if it is agreed upon by both.

It needn't be this angst ridden. It can be mature, sane and calm, depending on how and when the discussion is broached. If the conversation is begun sensitively and kindheartedly and in an appropriate place, there will be less difficulty.

Of course, if the person you're breaking up with has a bent for drama, anger and/or defensiveness, there will be yelling, name calling, perhaps even dish throwing. So make sure you do it in a public place where his behavior will be modified, or security can be fetched quickly. Also, make sure to meet him there so you have your own getaway car — I mean transportation. And changing the locks may be in order if he has a key to your place.

What are signs you should break up?

💙 You've become increasingly disenchanted with him. You no longer think his jokes are hilarious, nor his idiosyncrasies charming. You used to think his eating salad with his fingers was cute. Now you think it's gross.

💙 His behaviors are more irritating than ingratiating. His machine-gun-like laugh used to be amusing. Now it's immature. When he dismisses his forgetfulness with, "I have a sieve for a brain" it used to sound sweetly self-deprecating. Now you notice you hear it every time he conveniently "forgets" to do something you've asked.

💙 You let voice mail answer when he calls. You used to love his frequent calls. But now, the fifth call of the day to give a moment-by-moment report on what he's done since you last talked — an hour ago — has gotten old.

💙 You find you are disappointed or angry more than pleased with him. He doesn't keep his word, forgets important events, doesn't do anything to please you or show he cares.

♥ He is argumentative, belittling, condescending, controlling, paranoid, angry, verbally abusive, self-obsessed and/or downright mean. Cut loose now and don't accept him back, no matter how much he begs. Don't.

♥ You don't want to introduce him to your friends or take him to the office party. You can't imagine kissing him or making love to him one more time. Or still being with him in a month.

♥ You hear yourself thinking, "We would really be better just as friends," "This isn't working," or "We aren't a match."

These are all signs you should let him go. You're not doing him any favors by sticking around when you're really not into the relationship. And you're preventing yourself from finding someone more compatible.

You justify staying because "I love him." It takes more than love to keep coupledom working. You can love your dysfunctional uncle, your abrasive aunt, your alcoholic cousin. But would you choose someone with their behaviors as your mate, despite your love for them? I hope you answer no. You deserve someone who is functional, kind and sober. Love is not enough to stay in a relationship that isn't working unless you're both willing to work hard to turn it around.

In management, there is sage advice on the best

time to fire someone: The first time you think of it. Now I don't believe you should fire someone on the spot when the thought crosses your mind. I believe you should talk to him/her about the problem and see if the behavior shifts into an acceptable range.

The same is true with a beau. You need to talk about it if something isn't working for you — and the sooner the better. Don't let it fester. If he can't or won't shift and it's very important to you, then unless you can decide it's not important, he will never measure up. So don't ignore it when you hear yourself thinking, "I can't imagine being with this guy long term," "I'm just not attracted to him romantically anymore," or "I'd never marry this man."

Many years ago, I dated a man for over a year who I knew I'd never marry. We even lived together. I knew from his comments he expected we'd get married, although he never actually proposed. Finally, I had to tell him we weren't going to get married. Much yelling, crying and door slamming ensued. While it wasn't right for him to assume, it wasn't right for me not to correct him when he'd make marriage comments. I led him on and it was not right. I swore I wouldn't do that to anyone in the future, nor would I want it done to me.

So if releasing needs to happen, think how you can do it considerately and sensitively — and soon. Very soon. Then you can relax in the peace-of-mind pool.

They come, they go

When a friend asks about a suitor I've talked about but is no longer around, they seem surprised when I say "He's gone. They come, they go."

This is how it is in the dating world. You see someone a few times, then they lose interest or move on, but don't bother to tell you. I've learned not to take it personally; it just isn't a good match, even if I thought it might be worth more exploration.

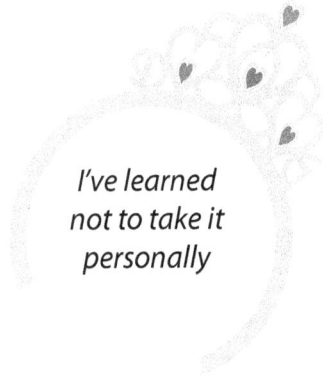

I've learned not to take it personally

I try to practice (but am not always good at) the Zen concept of non-attachment. I enjoy the time I am with someone, and if we continue to see each other and we're both enjoying it, great. But if one of us decides it isn't a good match, then fine. It truly isn't a good match unless both people feel so. I work hard not to leave a guy hanging, so I will either tell him personally, or if we've only met once, through an email. However, I find many, many guys just do a David Copperfield — they vanish.

I may write him an email if I am interested in staying in touch, but I most likely won't call. I figure he's moved on. He knows how to contact me, and if he's drawn to do so, he will. But I send a nice email to let him know I figure he thinks it isn't a match and if he'd like to reconnect at some time, he's welcomed to do so. Some guys think if too much time has passed, they are embarrassed to try to rekindle a relationship, so I want him to know the door is open, even if just as pals.

It can be hard to practice non-attachment if you are strongly drawn to someone. But if you become too attached too early, it leads to demanding, needy, controlling, jealous behavior — which will drive the subject of your desire to leave in a flash. So just enjoy what you have and you will, in fact, be more appealing. He will want to be around you because you have no expectations that he will call the next day or take you out the next weekend. It actually makes him want to be with you more.

But if he disappears, don't hunt him down. Just know he wasn't a good match for you and say what I've said very, very often: "Next!"

Hamstrung by your own integrity

Early in your relationship you both promised that if there was ever anything that bothered one of you so much to consider breaking up, that one would have the respect and courtesy to share this in person or at least on the phone, not in an email, text, IM or voice mail. Having been broken up with in each of these virtual vehicles by midlife men you'd dated for a while, you felt it was disrespectful.

You both agreed that you would share any concerns in person

Several months into your current relationship, your man went AWOL, not returning your calls, emails or texts. You had no idea where he was, or if he was OK. He had promised to make daily contact to check in, so after four days of silence you'd had it. You were ready to break up with him for his inconsideration and breaking his agreement — something that happened too frequently for your taste. You take your promises seriously and consider keeping or renegotiating commitments to be a sign of maturity, responsibility, and integrity.

But believe it or not, integrity can be a problem. Because you made the commitment to not break up without actually talking to him, you can't send him an "I've had it. We're done." email, text, IM or voice mail. You are hamstrung by your own integrity. You have to wait until you speak to him to tell him your feelings.

Friends say you shouldn't feel beholden to your promise because he isn't holding up his agreement to connect daily — and this isn't the first time he's broken an agreement. So that releases you from your vow. But you know that you need to act in accordance with your values no matter how badly someone else acts. You want to be able to live with yourself knowing you act in integrity even if someone else does not.

Then he texts you after several days with a plausible reason for his silence, even though you think any reasonable man who cared about you would have reached out sooner. His texts sweet talk you into releasing your ire.

Eventually it is he who ignores your mutual pledge and breaks up with you via text. This cements your observation that his promises to you meant little. So while you are sad because you liked him a lot despite the clear mismatch in values, you are also relieved because you know a relationship is doomed with someone who doesn't put integrity as a priority.

"You are just too much work"

Sometimes a guy says something that stings but it shifts your perspective so it ends up for the better.

We'd been seeing each other a few weeks. I enjoyed his company. Smart, funny and affectionate, he made me laugh like no one else. I thought it was going well. Then, over cocktails, he told me he didn't see us together long term. When I asked why, he uttered, "You are just too much work." Shocked and hurt, I didn't really understand what he meant.

You see, I consider myself a medium-maintenance woman. I'm not demanding about much. I'm not so low maintenance that a guy can just pop into my life when he wants and expect to pick up where we left off. But I also don't demand extravagant gifts, dinners, and 100% attention.

So when he said I was a lot of work, I asked what he meant. He said, "When I come home, I'm beat. I want a beer, a good meal, to watch the tube. You require conversation. And not just 'How was your day?' or 'Can you pick up the dry cleaning?' But real conversation that makes me think. I'm too tired at the end of the day to think like that. I just want to zone out."

While it stung that he thought I was a lot of work, he was right in that I do require a thinking man — someone who wants to participate in meaningful dialog. I wouldn't be happy with a couch potato "zoner" — someone who doesn't care about engaging in anything beyond trite conversation. Nor would I be happy with someone who couch potatoes every night in front of the TV, even if he's watching PBS or the Discovery Channel.

It stung that he thought I was a lot of work

What about you? Are you "a lot of work?" Are you low-, medium- or high-maintenance? And what, exactly, do each of those mean to you?

50 ways to leave your lover? 4 ways not to leave your suitor

If you know it isn't a good match, you owe it to him to tell him and then either move on or become friends. But do so graciously, respectfully and gracefully, no matter what. Here are four ways NOT to let him know.

💜 *Via email* — if you've dated him more than a few times, have the guts to tell him in person that you aren't going to see him again, or if that's not possible, by phone. I had a lover break up with me via email after we'd dated exclusively for 7 weeks. He said he was too cowardly to do it in person! It was disrespectful and hurtful to not do it in person when we'd seen each other just the day before.

💜 *After only a few minutes* — After 10 minutes one guy told me that he wasn't attracted to me so he was leaving. On one hand, it was good that he didn't waste either of our time. But he could have been more graceful than saying, "I'm not attract-ed." How uncouth!

💜 ***By IM*** — This is the modern version of the "Sex and The City" Berger breakup Post-It to Carrie. Tacky. A guy I dated for 6 weeks sent me an Instant Message breaking up with me — when he knew I wouldn't be around to read it until later. Essen-tially, it is as classless and spineless as an email.

💜 ***AWOL*** — Not returning emails or voice mails. I've had two guys do this, one I'd dated for 6 weeks. After talking 5 or 6 times a day for 6 weeks, he suddenly didn't respond to any emails, IMs or voice mails. He'd left some clothes at my house that I wanted to return to him after I didn't hear back for a few days, and he still didn't respond. I left them on his front porch, as there was not much else I could do.

Have the courage and decency to be gently honest when you release this person back into the dating pool. You will feel better about yourself, and you'll leave him not hating you.

Allow him to change his mind

omen complain about guys who suggest future plans or verbalize their affection in the early stages of dating. Then these women are irritated, nay, angry, when the guy disappears. It is easy to do, and I've found myself doing it, too.

Instead of labeling the guys "liars," "jerks," "losers," and "snakes," why not just label them "human"? Just accept that he changed his mind. After getting to know you better, he either reassessed his priorities or realized you two aren't as good a match as he thought at first. As people get to know each other, behaviors come out that may be deal breakers for the other. Of course, we hope he has enough respect for us and courage to let us know.

I'm not naive. I know some cads and players use the "future" ploy when trying to woo a woman. Many women like to hear that a guy likes her so well he's talking about future activities together, or says the things we like to hear. But my experience, and those of my friends, is that only maybe 10% — if that — of those we've gone out with are blowing smoke when they sweet talk us. You can usually tell those guys early on through email and phone conversations, so there's no need to actually meet them.

You've changed your mind about a guy after dating him a little while, right? Of course! The difference is when someone says things that imply he is thinking you'll be together weeks, months, or even years from now. You buy into it as all seems to be going well. You like him, too. And by all indications he feels similarly entranced. You want to be together, so you like it when he says things that sound like he plans to be with you in the future.

When you're clear he's changed his mind, instead of getting mad, be glad!

So when you're clear he's changed his mind, instead of getting mad, be glad! (Sorry for the altered old advertising slogan.) Be happy that he changed his mind now, even if he left you hanging and didn't communicate his change of heart. Imagine how much worse it would be if he had this revelation weeks, months or years from now, after you'd invested a lot of time and energy into the relationship.

When it is apparent something has shifted for him — he no longer calls, emails, or returns your calls — just release the feelings you had for him as well as the

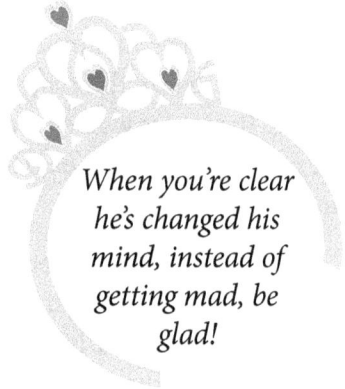

anger at his going "poof." He may not have told you, in part because he hadn't really articulated it himself or he was afraid of hurting you or creating a lot of drama for himself. (I still am amazed that men think going "poof" won't hurt the woman.)

So, accept his humanness (not to be confused with humaneness), complete with his ineptness at communicating, his herky-jerky way of moving on, and his exercising his option to change his mind. As you may have already experienced, this can happen in a marriage, not just in the early stages of dating, even after vows are said and commitments are made. I am not saying that I endorse this behavior or feel it is right, but I also know that you can make yourself bitter by being righteous and repel everyone in your path. So you can get angry that he disappointed you and has gone back on his word, or you can accept that unfortunately humans do that, work through your anger, and move on.

Breaking up is hard to do — right

In a *New York Times* article "Is It Over? Log on and See," journalist Melena Ryzik explores how many young people don't know their partner has broken up with them until they see his/her MySpace status changed to "single." She points out that the status change often quickly follows a spat — but sometimes it's too quickly. Sometimes within hours. And the other is shocked at the seeming finality.

Sometimes the status change is noted before a spat or breakup

However, sometimes the status change is noted *before* a spat or breakup. Ouch! One date told me he learned his girlfriend considered herself single when her profile appeared in his matches on Yahoo!Personals. While he'd hidden his profile and cancelled his membership, he still received a weekly list of matches. She showed up. He decided to do a little sleuthing so started another profile with a new identity. He emailed her, only to learn that she said she had broken up with her last boyfriend (him) and was now single. Interesting that she was still accepting his date invitations and hadn't bothered to tell him she was breaking up!

My experience is that few men (and I hear women, too) make a clean break. Many just stop emailing and/or calling after a few dates. While this isn't officially "breaking up" as we were never really going together, it does make me scratch my head. I'm told that men don't want to hurt a woman's feelings by telling her outright it's not a match. And they think disappearing is better? I've also been told they want to avoid any possible drama — yelling, crying, etc. — because, in a man pal's words, "Men are cowards." Of course, I understand women are often cowards, too.

So if you know you don't want to see him again, have the class and courage to just tell him you don't think you two are a fit and wish him well.

Why men go "poof"

anish. Disappear. Do a David Copperfield.

I've pondered this a lot, as it's happened often. I've interviewed men friends. The following is what I've gleaned.

If you don't hear from a guy after one date, it's clear he's not interested. No problem, even though it's classier to send a nice email stating such. But what if you've gone out 2, 3 or more times? You seem to enjoy each others' company. You have fun. Laugh. Good conversation. Some handholding. Maybe some kissing. Maybe more. Then poof. He's gone. Without a word.

Here are my theories on why he disappears

Here are my theories on why he disappears. He goes poof without so much as an "I'm not feeling it," "I thought we were a match, but now I don't think so," "I'm looking for casual dating and it seems you want more,"

"We want different things, so I don't think we should continue seeing each other," "I've decided to focus on someone else (or get back with my ex)," "You're a wonderful woman, but I'm not feeling chemistry," or "I just wanted a booty call."

💜 *He doesn't want to hurt your feelings*, and doesn't know how to say (in person, phone or writing) any of the above. So he thinks it's best to stop contact and hope you'll get the message.

💜 *He doesn't want any drama.* He's had experience — or heard stories — of otherwise reasonable women going ballistic when a guy cuts her loose. Lots of yelling, crying, blaming, name calling, insulting his manhood or ancestors, perhaps throwing items — at him, down stairwells, out windows.

💜 *He doesn't feel connected enough to you* to feel he owes you any explanation.

💜 *This is his pattern and it's worked for him in the past,* so he sees no reason to actually communicate with a woman he's been seeing and now decides to drop.

💜 *He doesn't like something fundamental about you* (your shape, kiss, laugh, personality) and he's afraid if he tells you he's moving on, you'll ask why. He doesn't want to have to tell you are a bad kisser/lover, have bad breath/BO, don't dress sexily, aren't smart enough, are too smart, etc. So to avoid an uncomfortable conversation, he disappears. (See "Broaching tough conversations," in the *Real Deal or Faux Beau: Should You Keep Seeing Him?* book.)

💚 **He doesn't feel he can satisfy you sexually.** One man told me that if there have been a few attempts and a man hasn't satisfied the woman he will leave, as he feels it reflects on him. So rather than face the possibility that he is a bad lover, or be humiliated if she tells him or tries to suggest changes, he'll leave. (See "An excuse to seduce or how important is sexual compatibility?" in the *From Fear to Frolic: Get Naked Without Getting Embarrassed* book.)

💚 **He doesn't think you can satisfy him sexually.** He has ED and wants you to put everything back the way it used to be. When he can't perform, you are history. He thinks there must be a sexy woman out there who can get it working again.

💚 **He doesn't think he can make you happy.** You have (or desire) a champagne lifestyle and he has a beer-budget job. He knows he can't give you what you want or expect, so he disappears into the night.

💚 **He prefers other priorities/activities** (work, sports, kicking with the guys) to hanging out with you.

💚 **He's involved with someone else.** He's auditioning you for spare gal (for when his alpha woman isn't available) or to replace his current one. He decides he's happier with his current squeeze. How would he possibly say that to you?

I'm sure women must vanish for similar reasons,

but since I don't date women, I don't know.

Why do you think men disappear without letting you know they're moving on?

Disposable dating

We live in a disposable society, where instead of fixing something, it is often easier and cheaper to throw it out and get a new one. Sometimes it appears this applies to dating as well.

With Internet dating there seems to be a steady supply of potential suitors. Even if you don't get contacted frequently, you can always search by your criteria and email as many men as you want. And some will respond.

So rather than trying to "fix" a budding relationship with frank talks, it seems much easier to just throw it out and get a new one. No fuss, no muss. Start anew. Get a fresh model.

There seems to be a steady supply of potential suitors

When one depended on meeting someone at work, the gym, through mutual activities or friends, people seemed to work a bit harder on relationship hiccups. Now that your love life can change with the click of a mouse, people are more inclined to jettison someone who isn't initially a fit. I know I've done this, reasoning why waste time trying to "fix" someone who doesn't want to be fixed. Move on to someone who's closer to what you're looking for.

I've moved on from all the men I've dated so far. I've recycled them back into the dating bin for another woman to discover. Just as garage sales are full of junk for the seller and treasures for the right buyer, so is the dating pool. Just because he's not right for you doesn't mean he won't be perfect for another.

So while I believe in working on relationships that have a great deal of potential, I also believe in recycling — men!

The choice: Break up or spend the weekend together

My friend shared his dilemma and his choice. A woman he'd seen a few times wanted to drive 2.5 hours from her home to see him. While he thought she had many wonderful characteristics, he knew they were not a match. He said, "I knew I had to break up with her then on the phone or let her come see me. I didn't have the energy to deal with the crying and upset of a breakup, so I let her come spend the weekend."

"But you're leading her on," I responded. However, I know I did the same thing at least once. "You wouldn't like to be led on. Now she thinks you're more of an item."

"You're right. But I just couldn't deal with the aftermath of breaking up with her. So now I've got to do it."

"And she'll be even more confused and hurt." I was trying not to chastise him, but instead help him see what he was doing to her.

Yes, breaking up often causes at the least some tears and candid conversation. At the worst, there is yelling, name calling, arguing, perhaps glass throwing. I took the coward's way out once — not returning a phone call from a suitor gone sour, then emailing him. I am not proud of this, as I prefer to act with courage and integrity and have at least a phone conversation to share my thoughts.

But I thought it was important for you to know that just because a man spends the weekend with you, it isn't necessarily an indication that he is deepening his relationship with you. Some men will do it for the companionship, the physical closeness, the sex. Some will do it because it is easier than breaking up. While women may do the same things for the same reasons, hopefully you wouldn't. Know that this is how some men operate.

Is my friend a cad, a player, a jerk? No. He is a caring, fun, intelligent, accomplished man. However, he — like most of us — can make short-term choices that are easier on him, without really thinking through the ramifications for the other person.

Managing disappointments

Dating can take an emotional toll. You get your hopes up when it seems someone is a great match. Even when you try to manage them, expectations creep in. You start having hopes, perhaps fantasizing about a future together.

Then something happens that dashes it all. A deal breaker emerges. A total impasse. Something one of you is not willing to live with. And it's over.

After spending 3 fun days together, nearly 24/7, he left with a promise to call that evening. He didn't. I felt something was amiss. Giving him the benefit of a doubt that he was too tired or forgot to call, the next morning I emailed him a nice note, saying I had a wonderful time and was looking forward to our talking. No response. At the end of the day, I called and left a voice mail asking him to call me back. Nothing. The next day I received a "have a nice life" email.

We won't go into how cowardly it is to send a blow-off email after nearly 100 hours we'd spent getting to know each other on the phone and in person. There is sadness, hurt and anger when you thought there was a possibility for a long-term romance that is shattered perfunctorily, without the honor of a conversation.

How does one manage disappointments?

It would be easy to blame and name call. I try to feel the hurt and sadness and let it be, rather than shrugging it off. If I bury the emotion now, it will come out inappropriately later. Allowing myself to feel the anger and pain helps me move through it more quickly than trying to suppress it. A good cry is often therapeutic. But be careful not to linger too long in sadness or you can get depressed.

After moving through the emotion, I remind myself that the person I am meant to be with wouldn't treat me this way. I look for the lessons from the encounter and vow to apply them to future interactions. I focus on the knowledge that what I learn from each guy is helping me complete the puzzle toward a great relationship. The most recent guy is but one puzzle piece toward the greater whole of a loving, trusting, growing relationship. The keystone piece — my match — has yet to appear. Some puzzles are simple, with only a few dozen pieces. Others have thousands. Let's hope mine is fewer than 100 — as I'm on to the next man!

How do you manage your disappointments?

Get back on the horse
that threw you

After a distasteful or painful dating experience, it's tempting to stop dating for a while. In fact, some people find a heartbreaking experience so odious that they swear off dating for years.

While it's a good idea to take a break to heal your wounds, if you go too long you lose your rhythm. You get rusty. It can affect your self-confidence. Yes, it is like riding a bicycle, the skills comes back. But sometimes it's hard to get your head back in the game.

If you go too long you lose your rhythm

My strategy is to take a little time to regroup, assess the lessons, refine what I want — and don't want — but then get back on the horse that threw me. If you don't, you're saying the setbacks win. You're letting a guy get you down who has undeveloped communication skills, lack of integrity, emotional unavailability, immaturity or who just realizes it isn't a match. You're letting his actions determine your happiness (or unhappiness). Don't give anyone that power.

Everyone has setbacks in life; it's how you deal with them that determines your future. If you let a few mishaps make you give up on finding the love you want and deserve, you are giving up on your future. Not all dates are fun and enchanting, although my experience is that only about 10% have been less than enjoyable. The great majority are unremarkable — not great, but not horrible. A few are heavenly, some resulting in equally sublime second and subsequent dates.

After an unpleasant experience, journal about the lesson(s) from it, take a bath, get a massage, go out with a gal pal, have a good cry, enjoy a little chocolate, go for a rigorous workout, attend a comedy club, update your perfect boyfriend's job description (in the *In Search of King Charming: Who Do I Want to Share My Throne?* book) — whatever it is you enjoy. Decide how long you will wait to get back on the dating horse. Maybe it's a few days, a week, or a month or two. But don't wait too long. Or the horse wins.

He wants romance; you want friendship

One of the hardest parts of dating is when one of you is interested romantically in the other, but it's not reciprocated. Whether you're on the giving or receiving end of "Let's just be friends," it's never easy to deal with. Here's my most recent trial with this situation.

Two years ago, we dated for 6 weeks. We parted amicably after I told him I wasn't "the one," which, by implication meant he wasn't my "one." We've kept in contact as each of us went into and out of relationships, but we never rekindled our romantic relationship. We'd email, talk on the phone, have an occasional dinner and movie, or I'd join him for a play or function. While each time I had a nice time, it cemented that I'd made the right decision not to see him romantically, as he had too many habits that drove me batty.

Friday, he asked me to attend a high-end business dinner that night. When we discussed the invitation, I made it clear I would be happy to attend as his escort, not his date. The distinction may be slim, but I wanted it understood that I had no romantic interest.

We had a great dinner and conversation with the dozen others present. Several couples assumed we were an item and invited us to dinner at their homes or on an outing. I didn't decline nor accept.

I purposefully didn't flirt with or touch my pal, as I didn't want to send any mixed messages. My attending this event was a friend doing a favor for another friend, just as I'd ask a male buddy to be my escort at an important function.

> *I didn't want to send any mixed messages*

On the way home we discussed some business challenges he was facing. I was fine giving him a free consultation. I liked that we kept the focus on business the whole time.

The following morning, I wrote him a brief thank-you email for inviting me to the event and introducing me to such interesting people. His response included:

"You are one very special woman that I appreciate. Last night I watched very carefully how you worked the room. Most who you contacted were very impressed and I can tell. This made me very proud.

"Frankly, I want you to be more than a friend. Sorry

*to be so blunt and unromantic; however this is what
I feel. For a long list of legitimate reasons I think
we could make it as a couple, as lovers, as support
mechanisms, as great companionship, as world
travelers, and have fun to boot. I am serious. I know
what I want."*

Drat! I had worked so hard to not give off any false signs that I may be interested in reviving our romantic relationship.

What do you think — can former lovers be pals? What if one wants to be lovers again and the other doesn't? Have you ever made this work?

Make sure to download your free eBook, "Dating Advice from XX Top Relationship Experts" at www. DatingGoddess.com/freebie

How to trump being dumped

To trump: outshine, outclass, upstage, eclipse, surpass, outdo, outperform; beat, better, top, cap; be a cut above, be head and shoulders above, leave standing.

A friend told me he'd been dumped by his last sweetheart and was still stinging from it many months later.

DG: What was the reason for the breakup?

He: It was stupid. Because I am fun and engaging with others, my sweetie felt I had the "potential" to cheat. I have never cheated, nor would I. This was all imaginary.

DG: Then your sweetie did you a favor by releasing you. Imagine your life with someone who was jealous about what you had the "potential" to do. This person would be easily riled at your making eye contact, smiling or talking to anyone else, even if you had no intention of cheating. Perhaps your partner would read your emails or text messages, or scrutinize your cell call log. You would live in an ever-present shroud of suspicion. Would you want to live with that?

He: No.

DG: Then in fact, you were done a favor by being released from the clutches of an insecure person, who would have made your life hell if you'd stayed together. How great that you now are available for a trusting, mature, sane person.

He: You sure know how to spin it!

DG: It's the truth, isn't it?

He: Yes, but I hadn't thought of it like that.

Most people don't. Although being released stings, if you can reframe it, you will be in less pain. There is always more than one way to interpret something, without being delusional. Both our interpretations describe the same outcome: He is single again. My philosophy is to choose the interpretation that leaves you most empowered, not depressed.

So was he dumped? You could say that. Was he released from a partnership with a needlessly jealous, insecure person? Yes. Both are true. Which one leaves him feeling best about himself and ready to meet a great person? The latter.

When you construe something negatively, ask yourself how else it could be interpreted. Choose the option that is still the truth but leaves you moving forward positively, not leaving you feeling less than.

When breaking up is a "Get Out of Jail Free" card

W hen we are not the one who ends a relationship, even a short-term dating relationship, it usually stings. Being on the receiving end of the boot with a longer-term, intimate relationship often creates wounds that last for years. No matter how much we work to accept it — and in some cases welcome it — the announcement from the other usually causes some pain.

In "How to trump being dumped" (page 41) I explored with a pal how being released from his overly suspicious lover was a good thing. But it's hard to see that at first.

Three months after my ex announced he was leaving, I was still in a lot of pain. One day while running errands and not thinking about the breakup, I heard a loud voice, as if someone were next to me in the car.

"You got a 'Get Out of Jail Free' card."

What was this disembodied voice talking about? I'm in my car, not playing Monopoly!

As I reflected on the message, I realized it was saying that by being released from my ex, I was being saved from the "jail" of continuing to live with a man who wasn't right for me — one who admitted he didn't think about me when I wasn't in the room. Who was, in his words, "emasculated" by my competencies.

I could have lived with him the rest of my life because I loved him and saw the positives in our relationship. However, he did not feel for me how I felt toward him. I deserved a partner who was equally in love with me and knew how to show it.

Also, since ours was not a vindictive divorce, neither of us was taken to the cleaners by the other. "Get out of jail free" meant that without a lot of drama or hideous expense, we could move on with our lives.

Some friends have shared their pain from past relationships gone sour. Some of these stories are heartbreaking. But you can easily imagine they could have been worse. You got out of the relationship — even if not by your initiation. You are now a wiser person, clearer on what you want, and unwilling to settle for what you settled for previously. You could still be with a guy who wasn't right for you. By moving on, you got a "Get Out of Jail Free" card. Now be grateful and move on to pass "Go" around the romantic version of the Monopoly game of life — even if you don't collect $200.

It's moving day!

Some Adventures in Delicious Dating After 40 readers have shared their unwillingness to move on from a love gone sour. Sometimes they know they need to, but they can't seem to cut that last emotional thread that leaves them feeling debilitated and unable to get on with their lives. Others seem to relish wallowing in retelling how the last guy did them wrong and how all men are immature liars and jerks.

Neither of these points of view are helping you get what you want — assuming you truly want someone who is good, kind, mature and respectful. Your point of view, and recounting it over and over and over, is repelling others. If it isn't, you're attracting men who commiserate about how his last love was a liar, cheat, etc. So you both are entering a potential relationship with a lot of negativity, not to mention suspicion. How hard is it to overcome someone's preconceived notion that the other gender is full of immature liars, which, by the way, they think you may be, too? They are on the lookout for anything that resembles the last person's immaturity, even though they may be misinterpreting your behavior. It's a vicious cycle.

So, in the interest of all Delicious Dating After 40 readers' good mental health, I declare today as

Moving Day!

Move on from those past hurts. Yes, grieving is something all of us need to go through, but have you been using grieving as an excuse a bit too long? Now, rather than it being a healthy part of ending a relationship, has it lingered so it is now so much of who you are you wouldn't know how to describe yourself without a "the last guy did me wrong" story in there?

Let it go!

The next time you're swapping relationship history with a gal pal or new guy, exercise self restraint and just say the last guy and you "didn't work out" or you two "wanted different things." That's it. No elaboration needed.

If you have remaining physical items that remind you negatively of him, get rid of them. Throw or give them away. When my ex left, I took down the gallery of our wedding pictures from the wall and put them in a box in the closet. Nearly all pictures of him were put away. If you need to rip up his photos or set them afire to feel closure, go for it (safely, of course). That lamp he gave you that you never really liked? Goodwill. That sweater he bought you but you felt it was too tight? Salvation Army. Get boxes for these things, as it is truly moving day! You are moving into the next great part of your life.

How to detect the end is near

Many midlife women have shared that they are blindsided, as I have been, when a man breaks up with them or just disappears. We are curious what signs we missed that the end was coming. Here are a few things I and others have noticed in retrospect.

- *He starts acting jerky.* A friend shared with me that when he wants to break up with a woman, he starts acting like a jerk so she'll break up with him. The reason he wants her to break up with him rather than the other way around is because there is less drama for him that way.

- *He calls less.* You can tell there's been a shift when he calls less frequently than in the past. He'd been calling every day and now starts skipping a day or two, giving you excuses why he "forgot" or "got busy." Once in a while this is okay, but if his daily calls are now every 2 or 3 days, look at it as a yellow flag.

💜 *He touches you less.* If you usually hold hands while walking, now he puts his hands in his pockets. If he usually puts his arm around you in the movies, now he holds his drink the whole time.

💜 *He doesn't talk about future plans.* There is no "Let's go to XXX this weekend," or "We should go see that new movie."

💜 *He neglects his grooming.* He no longer bothers to shave before seeing you, put on cologne, or wear anything other than old sweats. Yes, as you get more used to each other, couples usually relax their grooming habits. But now he never seems to want to look good for you.

💜 *He doesn't want to go anywhere.* Instead he wants to bring in a DVD and take out — or have you cook. He's not willing to invest any money in you and the relationship. You have been relegated to booty call.

💜 *He goes home after said booty call.* Not much cuddling, and no waking up together. So no spending the next day together.

💜 *He takes home his stuff.* If he kept a toothbrush at your place, or other personal items, they begin to go home with him until there's nothing left.

What have you noticed are signs that the end of the relationship is near?

Should you seek feedback on why it didn't work out?

'm sometimes asked why my multi-week relationships didn't work out. If the guy released me, I don't really know so can only guess. I've been asked, "What did the guy say when he broke up with you?"

The truth is, most of them have just gone poof, even after seeing each other 5-7 weeks. Very few men officially "break up" by communicating they don't want to see me romantically anymore. And if they do, they often use the nebulous, "It wasn't working for me."

When I've gently pressed and calmly said I'm really interested in what wasn't working, the answers have been unconvincing. After dating 7 weeks, I suggested to one beau that I'd love to meet his college-age kids sometime. He broke up with me soon after that (in an email) saying he just wanted to be friends. When I said,

"Okay. Can you tell me what precipitated this?" he said he wasn't comfortable with my meeting his kids this soon. Ironically, a few weeks later I arranged to return some of his belongings and one of his kids was home and he seemed comfortable introducing us. Go figure.

So I'm not convinced many men would tell a woman what was really going on, even if we didn't yell or cry, but asked calmly and patiently, not blaming.

The feedback I receive is nearly identical to the feedback I'd say to the giver

I've also noticed with uncanny regularity that when I've received "constructive" feedback from someone — not just suitors — the feedback I receive is nearly identical to the feedback I'd say to the giver. A colleague once told me that I "had rough edges" which is exactly how I had described him months earlier to someone who didn't know him. So I think sometimes we are mirrors for others who see their faults in us more clearly than they see them in themselves.

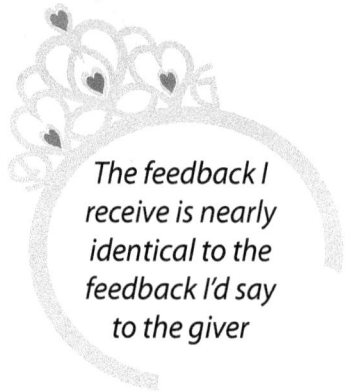

Does this mean you shouldn't try to get feedback in dating's equivalent of an exit interview? No. I encourage you to solicit feedback from former sweeties as well as close friends to see if they can shed light on your blind spots. If you get consistent feedback from dates, beaus, or friends, give it credence. A favorite question I ask my pals is, "How do you see me shooting myself in the foot?" They will help you see areas you sabotage your efforts.

In dating, you see people do stuff that you think, "If only someone would tell him — he would be so much more successful." You don't want to be that clueless person who keeps unknowingly repelling potential suitors. Remember on "Friends" Chandler's (Matthew Perry) love interest, Janice (Maggie Wheeler), with the obnoxious laugh? While I'm sure there are some people on the planet who wouldn't find it annoying, the majority do. If someone lovingly told her, she might be able to tone down the volume to a minimum.

In "I could really see us together if you lost weight" (in the *Assessing Your Assets: Why You're A Great Catch* book) I shared that I don't think you should expect someone else to change. But we're not talking about him now, we're talking about you.

Should you solicit feedback from all former love interests? I believe you should from the ones with whom you felt particularly matched. In my professional expertise of strategic customer service, I tell clients to pay closest attention to the feedback they receive from their best (by their definition) customers. You want to attract more like them, so you want to make sure you're not driving them away unwittingly. The same is true for beaus. You are most interested in feedback from the ones you felt had long-term potential — until they broke up with you.

When you receive their feedback, I'm sure you know you should strive to remain calm, not get defensive nor overly emotional. Should you begin yelling, sobbing or name calling? Not a good strategy. That will not gain you any useful information.

Even if some time has passed — in fact, some time passing is probably better — have the courage to contact those with whom you had a good relationship that went awry. Ask for feedback calmly and non-defensively. See if you can uncover some trends and make some modifications if you do. And try not to laugh like Janice.

What's your need for closure?

D o you need closure after you stop dating a guy? If you decide to end it with him, do you feel better if you let him know, rather than not returning calls or emails? If he decides to end it, do you want to have a final conversation, not just get an email or him going poof?

It seems more women than men I've spoken to want closure. My women friends want to know why or at least have a conversation that allows them to say (or hear), "You are terrific. I just don't feel we're a match."

More women than men I've spoken to want closure

I have a high need for completion, which is true in every aspect of my life. I like closure. I don't like things left dangling. However, with dating, some guys just disappear, not returning emails or phone calls. So

I make up my own closure. Often I just tell myself, "Oh well. We obviously aren't a match. Next!" That allows me to let go more easily and move on to the next guy in queue.

If you are like me, rather than obsessing about what went wrong and why he doesn't call, see what you can tell yourself to release any feelings of disappointment and resentment and just move on. Some people find it useful to write the guy a letter telling him what you want to say but not sending it.

How can you complete a relationship even if it is just within your own mind?

Being "thrown under the bus"

This is a common term in the dating world to express a breakup. At the end of a relationship, you are either the one being thrown or the one doing the throwing. Neither image is a pleasant one. When I suggest my sweetie is going to throw me under the bus, he cringes at the words.

Why is it that this has become such a popular term, given the violent image it conjures? It implies finality, where "He broke up with me" suggests there is chance for reconciliation.

Consider what other terms for a breakup communicate:

"He dumped me."

"He dropped me like a hot rock."

"He called it quits."

"He went poof."

All of these say the decision was solely in his hands. While it may be true that you wanted to continue and he didn't, you sound like a powerless victim.

We choose words to express our feelings and view

of reality. Some convey our sense of victimhood, that we had no say in the outcome. Others show a sign of humor, which means you aren't taking it too seriously.

Or you could want to telegraph that it was you making the decision, even if that wasn't the truth. So to pump your ego, you may say, "I dumped him." Which is not respectful of him. "I called it quits" proclaims that you were the sole decision maker.

If you use the term "throw under the bus," ask yourself what you are expressing. Are you feeling sad but attempting to be light about the situation? How about choosing a term to explain to your friends what happened that doesn't make you sound like a victim? Something like:

> "We parted ways."

> "We're not seeing each other anymore."

> "We decided we aren't a good match for each other."

> "We've moved on."

> "We decided to be just friends."

The point is, no matter how sad, upset, or disrespected you feel, express the breakup in terms that honor both of you, no matter how much of a loser, jerk and cad he was. You will show your class through your words, and you will have more respect for yourself.

After the breakup, what if you miss him?

No matter if you broke up with him or he with you, after a while — days, weeks, months — you may begin to miss him. The horrible things he said or did may fade and only the good parts are remembered. His sweet kisses, great sense of humor, thoughtfulness, and generosity are increasingly on your mind. It's called selective memory.

It's hard to remember that you broke up for a reason. If you called it quits, it was over some deal breaker that you thought was insurmountable. On reflection, you're now thinking maybe you were too picky, rigid or uncompromising. His foibles are now cloudy, but his assets are shining bright.

If he broke up with you, it was over something he felt was an impasse. Do you think he's had a change of heart? Do you believe if you promise to change, it will win him back? Perhaps. But he'd be contacting you if he wanted to explore it.

People — especially midlife people — have a difficult time making radical changes. It can and does happen, typically after some dramatic event like a health challenge or other wake up call. Or changes can occur after a stern talk with themselves or a loved one that their current life is light years away from what they want and they'd better make big changes now.

So, if you want him back, are you willing to make sustainable changes to fit what he says he wants? If you are highly motivated, then you can do it. However, most of us drift back into our old habits after a while.

Most of us drift back into our old habits after a while

If you were the one pulling the plug, if you get back together do you trust that he'll make the changes needed to satisfy you? Or are you willing to live with the former deal breaker(s)?

I broke up with a man I'd dated for 6 weeks early in my post-divorce dating life. I apparently did it gently, as we've kept in touch. Every 6 months we'll have dinner or see a movie. He has said he wanted us to be an item again, and I repeatedly tell him that I'm just interested in being friends. While I enjoy his company as a pal, every time I'm with him the things that got on my nerves come out again. Seeing him reinforces that I made the right decision. (See "He wants romance; you want friendship," page 37)

After dating a man for six months, I broke up with him for a variety of reasons. After a month, I'd met no one who was as attentive and I missed him. I was tempted to make contact, but I reminded myself why I'd cut it off. The issues that I found unacceptable weren't easily changeable, so I felt it was unfair to require those as a condition of our having a relationship. And they were not things I felt I could learn to live with. So I released him so another woman with different criteria could find him.

When I've been the person who was released, after the hurt wears off it can be easy to yearn for my former beau. My suggestion: don't make contact. Unless your breakup was over something really silly, don't give in to being drawn back into a relationship that he said good-bye to. That means it wasn't a fit for one of you, which means it's not a good fit. Period.

If the relationship ended amicably, you may be able to be pals, as long as you aren't secretly harboring a desire to get back together. That only makes you crazy. And when he starts dating someone else, it will put an impossible strain on your friendship.

So know that it is natural to miss him. Especially if you are lonely (or horny). But don't try to get back together. With very few exceptions, it will just elongate and exacerbate your heartache.

The anatomy of a relationship meltdown

My beau and I had a meltdown. It started over something dumb, but then escalated to yelling and disparaging remarks. This prompted me to rethink if I was willing to continue with someone whose company I enjoyed, but knew there were some big deal breakers. As much as I tried the techniques I've suggested to you, I was unable to put them aside.

I've looked at my contributions to the meltdown, as well as his. I am not without error. I made mistakes. In our last two phone conversations, I yelled back at him when he began yelling and making inaccurate statements about what I felt and thought and my motivations. But in reviewing the emails of this meltdown, I never got accusatory nor affronted him personally.

I asked a former beau who I'd dated last year for 2.5 months if my latest guy's accusations paralleled his impressions so I'd know if I was misperceiving my actions or if my beau was filtering them through his own past wounds. I was assured that he had never seen any of what the beau described. Was it that I never behaved as the beau said, or that I just didn't act that way with my former guy?

So what happened? The details are unimportant. In "The first fight" (in the *Ironing Out Dating Wrinkles: Work Through Challenges Without Getting Steamed* book) I talked about the importance of noticing the three parts of the fight process: before, during and after. In this case, all parts spoke volumes. I saw behaviors in him I hadn't seen before. While we sometimes say things we regret in the heat of anger, I don't believe we say things we don't mean. I think we speak our naked truth during this time, as our social filter is removed. We say exactly what we think, so you get to see an unmasked view of the person's perception of you.

I don't believe we say things we don't mean

His unscreened view of me was so loathsome I knew that even if we got through this, I'd always know he interpreted my behaviors in the worst possible way. How could you continue to date someone you knew put up with what he considered odious behavior flaws? Could I ever feel I could be myself knowing nearly everything I said or did was being misconstrued? I didn't envision this as the way I wanted to live my life.

So while it was he who said "I'm done," I didn't try to dissuade him from his decision. As it is, I've endured a stream of scathing emails. If it was I who pulled the plug, I imagine the stream would have been a river. I now understand why some men just go poof — if they think their trying to talk rationally with someone will result in irrational blistering vitriol. And I'm reminded of "When breaking up is a 'Get Out of Jail Free' card" (page 43).

How you know you're over a guy

One of you has called it quits. If it is him, you may harbor lingering hopes he'll IM, text, email or call you. This delusion may last days, weeks, months, or even years. Even if you pulled the plug, you may secretly hope he'll see the error of his ways and apologetically come back. So you keep his lines of contact open.

When you're clear you're done, however, you delete his roads to your heart. Depending on his preferred methods of communication, you begin to sever the ties.

- You delete him from your IM Buddy list and block contact.

- You remove him first from your speed dial, then from your cell phone list altogether.

- You erase any pictures of him on your cell phone.

- You take him off your email contact list.

- You may set up his email to go on your "bozo" list, automatically putting any future emails in your trash.

💜 If you found him on an online site, you remove him from your favorites, then block him from contacting you through the site.

💜 You put or throw away any snapshots you have of him.

💜 As discussed in "It's moving day" (page 45) you give away any items he gave you that you don't really want.

💜 If you have any of his belongings, you arrange to return them through a friend or mail, or donate them to charity.

You feel no sadness, remorse or delight when you take these actions. You are merely removing someone from your life with whom you desire no further contact. You don't wish to be reminded of him, so you don't want to stumble upon his name in your address book or picture on your screen saver.

You're creating space for someone wonderful to enter your life. The more you are surrounded by reminders of people who elicit hurt or sad feelings, the less space you have in your psyche for positive, loving feelings, which any new guy will pick up.

So know by cleaning out reminders of love gone awry you are making space for a wonderful new love.

The truth-telling

session

Should you tell a guy you've dated but released what drives you batty about him, so he can fix it so it won't bother future love interests?

Yesterday, my first post-divorce beau emailed asking if I'd give him honest, specific feedback on what he did which may be repelling other women like me. It's been three years, but I can still remember many of the issues.

I asked if he was sure he wanted to know the details. He said yes. I told him we should discuss this face to face, not email. He was anxious to meet to discuss this as soon as possible.

Now I'm in a quandary. Do I tell him all the specifics that drove me to break it off with him? Or just the major ones? I've provided executive coaching for years and had to tell a very intelligent man he needed to wear ironed shirts, among other things. I've had to tell others what no one else was comfortable telling them. So I'm not without skills in this area. However, telling an old flame has a different feeling. I want to be sensitive to his heart and ego, yet give him enough information that he can modify his behaviors if he chooses to. And I will couch my comments in that other women may have different hot buttons than mine.

He wants to attract intelligent, successful, caring, loving, active women. Do I need to tell him the obvious: that he's 100 pounds overweight and would have a better chance if he shed some? Or is this too insulting? He lists himself as "athletic" in his online profile, although he has trouble walking more than a few blocks.

He works alone and does most of his business through email and phone. However, he dons business attire for networking functions and conferences. The last few times I've seen him in this garb, his jackets were ill fitting and the shirtsleeves too long. Since he doesn't

His jackets were ill fitting and the shirtsleeves too long

see these issues, I'll suggest he visit his tailor.

There are more issues that are irritating habits which would be off-putting to others, I'm sure. He commonly worked on the computer when talking to me reading me, parts of emails from people I don't know and don't really care about. He'd IM me frequently during my work day for nothing but chatter. His emails were often poorly written — I thought he had English as a second language when reading the first one he sent.

There are other values issues that were a mismatch for me. He seems obsessed with status, insisting on a high-priced car, season theater tickets for several companies, season tickets for local sports teams, fine dining, expensive wine collection, private club membership and fancy vacations even though he had nearly no savings and is 60 years old. I have no trouble with the trappings of success if one can afford them. He spent all that he earned and had very little set aside for retirement.

Have you ever had a truth telling session with someone you've dated? If so, did you limit your feedback to just the key issues, or did you let him know all the details?

DatingGoddess.com

Failed relationships' blessings

A friend and I were discussing failed relationships. She said, "It depends on your definition of 'failed.' Not all relationships are meant to be long term. Sometimes you are pulled to be with someone for a short time to learn the lessons each of you has to offer the other, then move on."

I saw the wisdom of this philosophy. It certainly reduces the time you'd spend being bitter, angry and sad when a relationship ends. Instead, you can focus on the lessons you learned about yourself and relationships, rather than being resentful and depressed, even if you initiated the break up.

In "'Is that so?' — A lesson in non-attachment" (in the *Date or Wait: Are You Ready for Mr. Great?* book) I shared a Zen story about accepting whatever is, without the teeth gnashing that often accompanies break ups. This concept is much easier to comprehend than it is to apply. If you thought the relationship was for the long haul, you'd planned a future together, and declared your love for each other, it is natural to feel grief when it ends.

By embracing my friend's philosophy it doesn't mean you can't grieve for the now-dashed hopes and plans for the future. But it does allow you to shift your mood more quickly and move on.

A 56-year-old friend told me of the only man with whom she ever lived. They were deeply in love, so she agreed to cohabit, something she'd avoided with previous beaus. After a few months, he announced he was moving out and leaving her. Her response — at least in this telling of the story years later — was, "Okay. I'd like your stuff gone by midnight. Whatever is here tomorrow will go to charity." That was it. Matter of fact. No yelling, name calling, china throwing.

> *It doesn't mean you can't grieve for the now-dashed hopes and plans for the future*

When she shared her calm response to something many of us would be hugely upset by, I asked her how she could be so unaffected. She said it wasn't that she was callused. She was saddened by his decision and his lack of communication about his feelings before his announcement. However, she knew it would be futile to try to change his mind, so yelling would let off steam, but if he didn't want to be with her, it would be silly for her to try to convince him. She only wanted to be with someone who wanted to be with her, too.

She learned a lot about what it takes to be in a full-

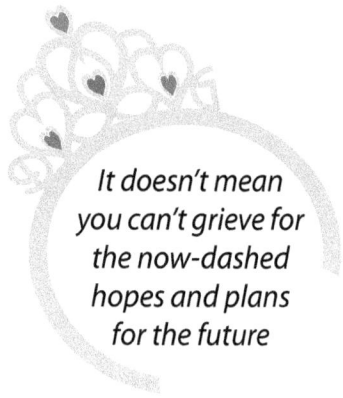

time relationship. After this experience, she decided she prefers to have her own living space, even if she is in a long-term relationship. She got clarity on what works best for her and was grateful for having shared the time with him.

Can you look back on "failed" relationships and list the blessings that they brought? The insights, learnings, decisions you made that have served you now? What lessons have these brought you?

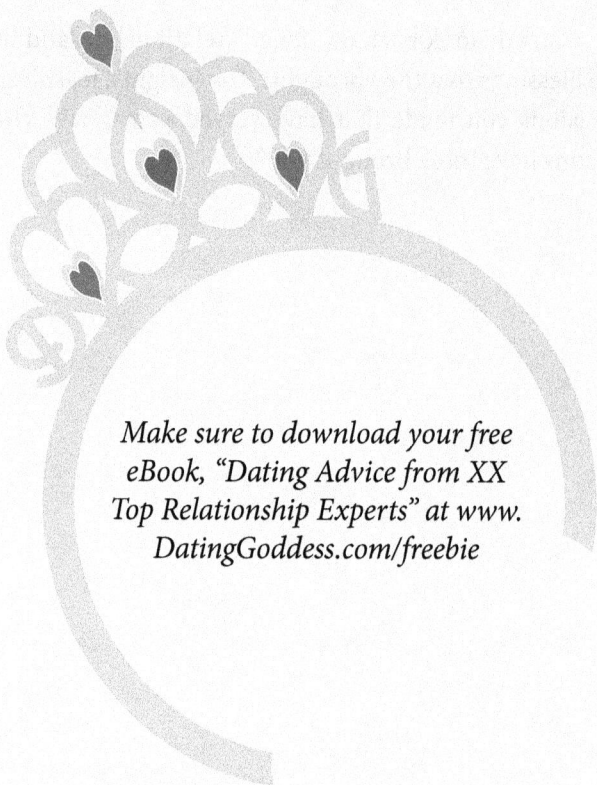

Make sure to download your free eBook, "Dating Advice from XX Top Relationship Experts" at www. DatingGoddess.com/freebie

"*Disruption precedes discovery*"

Keynote speaker Ian Percy uttered these words as a way to explain that what he was about to say would be disturbing to some of us in the audience. In fact, he said, some of us would not like what he said at all. But his purpose was to shake up our thinking a bit. And he did.

I, of course, saw this comment as relating to dating. "Disruption" is when we go through a divorce or intense breakup. Our routine is disrupted. Our thinking is disrupted. Our self-definition is disrupted. Instead of being wife/girlfriend/mate/life partner we are now "single," "unattached," "divorced" or even "widowed."

"Disruption" is when we go through a divorce or intense breakup.

One of the biggest challenges for me immediately

after my ex said he was leaving was facing the loss of my roles. I would not — at least in the immediate future — be wife, lover, partner. What would I be to his son — his ex-stepmother? How about to his newborn daughter — ex-step-grandmother? Her grandfather's former wife? I grieved for the part of my identity that was changed.

After we mourn the loss, however, that disruption can cause discovery — self-discovery. Reassessing who we are and what we want. Discovering anew what kind of person we are now. Redefining ourselves. And often reinventing ourselves in the process.

In the case of my titles, my step-son assured me I would always be a part of his family, and he wanted his daughter to know me. He invited me to continue to stay connected. It brought us closer.

So instead of cursing disruptions in your life, look at them as a time to rediscover who you are now and what makes you happy now, instead of who you were when you began your relationship.

When I recovered from my marriage's dissolution, I found freedom and excitement in reexamining what I wanted in my life and in my next relationship. I did not want the same things as the 28-year-old who entered the relationship with my ex. I got to reinvent myself as the single woman I wanted to be.

What discoveries about yourself have disruptions in your relationships created for you?

"Why Men Leave Home"

watched the 1951 B-film "Why Men Leave Home." I was interested to see what messages women were given a half-century ago about beauty and relationships, and how these messages have changed — or not.

The plot in a nutshell: a "dowdy" woman puts housework ahead of putting out. Her handsome doctor-husband won't stand for her not performing her wifely duties, so despite having a 10-year-old daughter, he leaves her. The wife makes the acquaintance of a Hollywood makeup artist who helps her see that if she doesn't pretty herself up, hubby's going to take up with his sexy nurse and divorce her. She sees the error of her ways, the makeup man gives her a makeover and her husband comes back to his

The makeup man gives her a makeover and her husband comes back

now-stunning wife.

This film is described as "an instructional primer for women regarding how to keep their husbands faithful."

Several lessons emerged:

- If you don't keep yourself beautiful and sexy, he'll leave you
- In addition to household duties, you must regularly perform wifely duties
- There are always other beautiful women to tempt him
- Only through the use of heavy makeup and stylish hair can you be attractive
- Having happy children, a clean home, home-cooked meals and a devoted wife is not enough to satisfy a man

While we have evolved as a society, as I read this list, I'm afraid many of these lessons are still true for many marriages. There are exceptions, of course, but these messages are still ingrained in many of our psyches, especially for those over 40.

What do you think? Have we moved past these 50-year-old clichés? Or are they still embedded in our brains?

The sting of rejection

Unless you have really thick skin, nearly all rejection has a little sting, even from someone in whom you aren't really interested!

If you email a guy and he responds, even with a nice "Thank you, but we're not a match," that has a mosquito-size sting. You're over it in a nanosecond. You might not even notice.

If you've talked on the phone and he either doesn't call again or sends an email saying he doesn't feel a spark, that hurts a little bit too. Like hitting your elbow on your desk. You barely notice.

You go out to dinner with someone after a nice phone conversation. You have an enjoyable time, although you are thinking he's a very nice guy but you're not feeling a spark. However, you have been advised that often there isn't a spark until the second or even third date, so you're willing to have another encounter. At the end of the date he hugs you and gives you a quick kiss on the lips.

You send him a nice email thanking him for dinner, telling him the qualities you liked in him, and saying you're open to another outing if he'd like. You get a nice email in response saying he could see you as a friend, but there was no romantic spark.

Ouch. Not a big ouch, but an ouch. It stings a little even though you didn't feel drawn to him. Why does it smart a little? You knew there wasn't a big draw on your side, so why should it hurt at all?

My theory: Because it was he who said "there's no attraction," not you. Silly, in a way, because the end result is the same. So why does it matter who pointed out the pink elephant in the living room? Neither of you felt "it" so why should it sting at all? Heck, this was much less painful than dental work, stubbing your toe hard, or falling off your bike. But the ego gets a tiny bruise just the same.

But I think most of us would rather have some closure, even if there's some brief discomfort, rather than not hear anything.

The key is to not wallow in the pain. Feel it, notice it, and then move on. Remind yourself that it is good that this happened now, as you could have wasted time thinking about and trying to set up another encounter when there really wasn't a spark. Let it go.

Put a bandaid on your ego, if necessary, and move on. Athletes with injuries much worse than this keep playing the game. They don't give up because they're clear on their priorities.

Next!

Forgiveness is key

In Elizabeth Gilbert's bestselling book *Eat, Pray, Love* she describes the year she took off to explore pleasure and devotion. She chose to spend 4 months each in Italy, India and Bali to immerse herself in what each place did best. In Italy she studied Italian and ate (gaining 23 pounds from pasta and pastry). In India she prayed and studied at an ashram. In Bali she focused on balance.

She had no intention of falling in love along the way. In fact, she'd promised herself she'd be celibate the whole year. But good intentions and promises were seduced away by a loving, sincere man.

The part that is relevant to Adventures in Delicious Dating After 40 readers is that she realized she could only be open to the love she unconsciously craved if she forgave herself and her past loves for whatever needed to be forgiven. Throughout much of the book she has

She forgave herself and her past loves for whatever needed to be forgiven

recurring upset about her marriage's painful dissolution and a subsequent intense love affair. No matter how much she enjoyed herself in Italy or how much she meditated and prayed in India, the old wounds kept surfacing. Only after a concentrated session of forgiving everyone involved was she able to become the person that attracted and allowed in a loving, sane, mature man.

What this illustrates is that if we have bitterness in our heart from any past loves, it will keep others at a distance. By forgiving yourself and them, you allow space for a great one to appear.

I don't know what you're planning to do tonight before you turn out the light, but I'm planning to turn up the volume on my forgiveness practice.

Are you holding on when you should let go?

Have you been in (or perhaps are in) a relationship that the other person isn't as into? It doesn't have to be a committed relationship, as this can happen even in dating. You are more into him than he is to you. He indicates this by his lack of calling, initiating outings, or verbally giving what you need. But you are into him, so you hang on for dear life and keep him around by giving him what you know he wants.

Soon after my ex announced he was leaving, I had a prophetic dream that painted a perfect picture for my (and perhaps your) situation. We were on a very tall bridge. He was hanging off the side. I was safe on the bridge behind the railing, hanging on to him with all my might, not wanting him to fall. I was crying, clutching at him, trying to bring him back topside.

He was saying, "Let go. It's OK. This is what I want." Finally, he slipped out of my grasp and fell down, down, down. About halfway a parachute appeared out of his backpack and he floated peacefully to the ground, having had the experience he wanted. Feeling relieved that he was safe, I turned around and entered the limo awaiting me.

This image allowed me to see that I was holding tight onto him, as I didn't want to let him go, even though it was clear he wanted to go. I thought he wasn't going to be safe since I didn't know about the parachute on his back. I didn't want him falling to his death. But he didn't get to the dangling position by accident — he purposefully put himself there. By letting him go, we both got what we wanted. He got the freedom to experience life as he wanted, unencumbered by anyone. I could have a life that he never wanted but I did.

So letting go when someone obviously doesn't want to be with you will bring you both more happiness. Sometimes our nocturnal dreams are clear indications of our waking dreams and reality.

Have you held on when you knew you should let go? What happened when you cut the tie?

Gently telling him you want to be friends

An Adventures in DeliciousDating After 40 reader asked:

> *Any ideas on how to gently let a good man go? I had several dates with a kind, intelligent, respectful man. We had much in common but by the third date it occurred to me that what we had was friendship, not a romantic attraction. He had different feelings that I was unaware of. I decided it was best to let go rather than lead him to believe I was interested in developing a relationship. I feel badly about this and if it should happen again, any tips?*

This is always a difficult question for anyone who dates with sensitivity and caring for the feelings of the other person. Here are a few ideas I've found effective when I've delivered this communication.

💜 If you've only had a few dates, as you have with this gentleman, you can have this conversation on the phone or even in email. I've often sent an email after a first or even second encounter when I realized the guy wasn't a match. I've said something like, "You are an intelligent, interesting, fun guy. However, I didn't feel the spark I know I need to explore a romantic relationship. But I'd like to have you in my network of friends. Would that be OK with you?" Most often the response is "Sure." Occasionally I've received, "I have enough friends," which is fine, too.

♥ If you've seen each other more than a few times, work to talk to him in person, assuming you live within a comfortable distance. If you are dating long distance, then have a live phone conversation, don't leave it on voice mail. And never do it via email or worse, text or IM. And if you live a distance apart, don't wait until he visits to tell him, as he will have gone to considerable trouble and expense to see you expecting to be pursuing you romantically. If you want to deliver the message in person, you should travel to him.

> *If you want to deliver the message in person, travel to him*

♥ When you are with him, don't do anything physically that would make him think you feel differently. So don't initiate hand holding, lingering hugs, or passionate kisses. If he tries to kiss you passionately, break it off quickly and turn your cheek.

💚 Arrange a meeting like coffee or a drink, not dinner. If the expectation is a longer outing, you will be worried about when and how to deliver the "let's be friends" statement and will be on edge. A shorter encounter also allows him to leave quickly if he is upset at your decision.

💚 Think carefully how you want to express yourself. Avoid the clichéd "It's not you, it's me." Some people think telling him what a great guy he is will only confuse him when you tell him you want to be friends, as he may think, "If I'm so great, why doesn't she want more?"

💚 When I've delivered the "let's be friends" talk, I didn't say, "I'm not sexually attracted to you," but instead said, "While I have grown fond of you, I realize that fondness is as a friend, not a sweetheart." If he responds as one man did, "Well, good relationships always start with friendships," escalate your language to be even clearer. "I am not The One for you, so it would be unfair to continue as if we are going to be romantic." If he insists that he does indeed think you are The One for him, you have to be blunt, as he's not getting the gentler wording. "As good of a guy as you are, I'm clear you aren't The One for me. But you have many qualities I enjoy, which is why I'm wondering if we could be friends." Or "I just don't think we are a match. But I'd love to stay connected as friends, if that would work for you."

How blunt you have to be will depend on how quickly he gets the message. If he is insistent that you are a good match, you will have to be more explicit, while still trying to be sensitive to his feelings. If he continues to not get it, you may have to just say, "I'm not romantically attracted to you, but I would love to stay your friend, if that is comfortable for you." One man said, "No, if you can't be my sweetheart it is too hard to have you in my life knowing I can't have you."

How have you found it best to deliver the "let's be friends" talk? What's worked for you? Or not worked when you've been on the receiving end?

Prince Considerate breaks up — considerately

We'd dated 3.5 months. He was the most considerate man I'd dated. So I dubbed him "Prince Considerate."

After dinner and a nice stroll, we settled back in my house for a DVD. But before we could get started, he pulled me to his lap and put his arms around me.

"This is a very hard thing, but I need to say it. I don't know why, but I'm not finding myself falling in love with you."

"I'm not finding myself falling in love with you."

He'd mentioned this a few weeks before, so it wasn't news. We'd both felt similarly, but knew the other person had a lot of terrific characteristics so thought we should give it a bit more time.

We talked about how neither one of us could

89

understand why we weren't moving along in the relationship — we both liked, respected and cared for the other. But the loving feelings weren't developing. We joked that perhaps the other wasn't dysfunctional enough for us to relate to some old patterns.

He said he felt he needed to bring this up now because we'd planned to spend New Year's Eve together (a week away), and he was feeling out of integrity. He didn't feel right about acting like we were in a relationship when we weren't really. While I didn't feel that celebrating New Year's Eve together meant we were in a relationship, I didn't argue.

Of course, the way he brought this up — sensitively, maturely, and respectfully — made me more fond of him. Did it make me love him? No. But I did think, "What a rare emotionally mature man." Which I already knew, but this was one more example of his being congruent.

I am oddly sad. I don't fully understand why. It wasn't as if I was in love with him, either. But it is a loss of his regular presence in my life, his thoughtful and generous gestures, his insightful observations. However, like many of my treasures, we promised to keep in touch.

He's broken up with you — he just didn't tell you

My guy pals have told me that men are emotional cowards. They'd rather walk barefoot over broken glass than do something that would make a woman cry. Thus their preference for going poof rather than tell you they have changed their mind.

A year ago I was interviewed by the *Wall Street Journal* for a story about how younger people learn their sweetie has broken up with them by their partner changing their Facebook relationship status to "single," or by a text message. I thought that was immature. Midlife people didn't do this kind of cowardly thing, did they?

Today I learned that my beau of 2 months has broken up with me. Did he tell me? No. In fact, in an hour-long IM two days ago he said, "I did not contact you nor meet you with the intention of our sharing a short-lived transient relationship. I am one who likes things to last for a very long time. Candid with you I will always try to be."

Well, so much for being candid! Here's how I learned that we are not the couple I thought — and he said — we were.

So much for being candid!

He had been gone for 2.5 weeks dealing with the aftermath of an unexpected family tragedy. We texted regularly and he called once. We both proclaimed our affection for the other and how much we missed each other. In the last month I regularly received messages like:

"My whole life has changed, oh what a wonderful change it is to be a part of your life and to have you be in mine. You enchanted me from the beginning and now I care not to think of being without you my sweet. Whether near or far you're always on my mind and in my heart because for you there is a special place reserved just for YOU." And, "Being away from you for any reason will not ever be enjoyable for me. You have a special place in my head and my heart and nothing I could here now imagine will alter that in any way because I tell you with pride and joy that I want YOU!"

We'd had the conversation about not being interested in seeing others, how we'd taken down our profiles from the dating sites, how we weren't pursuing or accepting invitations from others. We didn't use the "exclusive" word, but we said it in different ways.

In the most recent IM conversation he disclosed he was going on an extended road trip the next day to clear his head — with no mention of our seeing each other before he left. He had no idea how long he'd be gone — it could be weeks. I was disappointed and hurt. As diplomatically as I could, I asked when we would see each other. When he returned.

In the past two months when we have been apart and I missed him, I enjoyed reading his hidden, now-private dating profile on the site where he found me. I've told him I do this, so he knows I read it periodically.

On the day we met, he hid his profile from pubic view and changed his headline from "Need Just You" to "I have found you." Under "How would you describe yourself," he'd changed "One happy man who sought to find that one good woman" to "One happy man who sought to find that one good woman to make my queen and by fate's will [my screen name] has come into my life now and I have no urge to seek another." And from "I am looking forward to meeting you and exploring more than possibilities. It is my hope that you are of a like mind" to "Lovely [my name], now that we've begun to communicate I am looking forward to meeting you and exploring more than possibilities. It is my hope that you are of a like mind."

When I looked at his profile this morning,

1) it was active again,

2) he had been on the site within the last 48 hours,

3) the headline and verbiage were back to the original.

In his most recent IM he mentioned one of the places he will visit is the small town where his last girlfriend lives. On our fourth date he said he'd told her about me and she wasn't happy. Well, it appears he will be seeing her on this trip — and by all indications it isn't to shout his love for me while jumping on her couch.

He had removed her pictures from his public Flicker account soon after we met. Now her pic is back. There were two of him and me — one of us kissing. Now that one is gone, although there is one left. Perhaps she, too, peruses his pics periodically, and he knows that she does, as he knows I do.

So all of this adds up to a cowardly man and a disappointed, single goddess. Unless I am misreading all this evidence.

Have you ever discovered someone you were dating exclusively broke up with you but didn't tell you? How did you handle it?

What's your relationship
recovery time?

"Recovery time" is however long it takes one to re-turn to normal after an event, whether it's the time it takes an athlete's body to return to normal heart rate or hydration after a grueling event, or some-one's return to health after a setback. Or how long it takes for someone to recover after a relationship's ending.

When I was first divorced I was told it would take 25% of the time I was married to recover and be ready for a serious relationship. I was married for nearly 20 years, so that meant it would take 5 years! I was incredu-lous. I didn't want to wait five years to find my next LTR. But here it is at the five-year mark and I feel I'm truly ready. I had too much healing and growing to do.

I don't know if the 25% rule of thumb applies to short-term relationships as well, but my experience is the more emotionally attached you were, the longer it takes to get over. If you find you are grieving the loss longer than the relationship lasted, something else is going on. I posit you're not just grieving that relationship, but perhaps the hopes and dreams you had for a future with someone you thought was a great match. And now the daunting task of finding someone else to help fulfill your dreams is heartbreaking.

Just like a champion athlete's body, I think the mark of an emotionally healthy person is how quickly one can recover from a breakup and get back to normal. That is not to say you shouldn't grieve — I think it's healthy to go through the stages of loss and feel what you feel fully, without trying to say you're fine when you're really not. But if you linger too long in denial, anger, bitterness or pain, you are not doing yourself any good.

How long should one grieve the loss of a promising relationship? It will vary with each person. But I think you should be conscious of if the time you're spending being resentful, angry, etc. is more than 25% of the relationship's length, you need to shift and let it go. If you need help from a counselor to do so, get it. The longer you wallow the less time and energy you'll have to focus on what you want next. And frankly, you're not any fun to be around in this state so no one new will be drawn to you.

If you are still holding on to anger about a breakup — recent or past — how can you let it go to complete your recovery?

Releasing revenge

I n a seminar I was leading, a customer service provider was irritated by the rude customers she dealt with daily. "I want to know how to get back at them," she demanded of me.

When someone has wronged us, it is common to want revenge. When a man has led us on, then unceremoniously dumped us without the courtesy of a call or explanation, it hurts. Bad. We want to lash out at him. We want him to hurt, too.

When we hurt, we want the person who caused our anguish to be in pain. And we're most willing to be the source of their pain!

But revenge accomplishes nothing. Maybe it makes you feel better short term. But since I believe in dating karma I think that the person who harmed you will get his due. It is not up to you to provide his comeuppance.

As I told the woman in the seminar, try to put yourself in his shoes. We have no idea what is going on with him, what past hurts have been triggered by you. All we know is he is not coming from a very high self to treat you this way. You can choose to stoop to his low level and retaliate, or you can take a deep breath, feel some compassion for the pain he must be in to treat another human being so badly, and wish him the best.

Hurting others usually comes from pain. I vividly remember hitting my head hard on a low-hanging door frame when visiting my favorite auntie. Immediately afterward she meant well by saying, "Careful." The pain was intense and I wanted to lash out, "What a stupid thing to say after I've bashed my head!" But I knew that was her way of wanting to be helpful. I was a hair's breadth away from lambasting one of the people dearest to me because I wasn't thinking clearly. Perhaps getting close to someone romantically triggered deep wounds for him that you'll never be privy to.

Can you honestly say you've never treated anyone, ever, at any time, badly?

You may be thinking, "I would never treat someone like that!" However, can you honestly say you've never treated anyone, ever, at any time, badly? You've never been inconsiderate or rude to anyone in your life, whether family member, friend or stranger? If so, I want to touch your hem. Most of us, even if rarely and unintentionally, have treated someone poorly. When you put it in this perspective, it is easier to have some compassion.

You may run into the man who wronged you in

jointly frequented places. You don't have to hold a grudge. When you see him, you can simply say "hello" and keep moving. Or when you think of him and start to get angry at how he treated you, instead see if you can be appreciative that he is no longer regularly in your life. Release the thought of anger and replace it with one of hoping that he gets what he needs to break through his past patterns of behavior that alienate him from good people like you. And try not to sound condescending when you say this to yourself!

Feelings of desired revenge only fester in you, raising your blood pressure, prompting tenseness, and causing you to wallow in a mental state that you don't want to stay for long. You can acknowledge your desire for him to be punished, but move through that feeling quickly. He will get what he will get — and he may not appear to ever be punished or change his ways, leaving other forsaken women in his wake. And unless he's done something illegal, it's not up to you to be the magistrate.

Requiem of a relationship

Today would have been my twenty-second wedding anniversary. I think it is important to reminisce about long-term relationships gone awry as one would at a memorial of a difficult person. Not dwell on the downs, but the ups. Paint a picture of what was added to your life as a result, not what was stripped. Focus on the lessons you learned about yourself, even if those came as the result of humiliation, pain, and bitterness.

So I ponder the gifts, the lessons, the treasures I will carry with me to my next relationship and my life. You don't have to wait for an anniversary to do this exercise. You could do it now. Especially if you find yourself holding onto some bitterness, it's best to do it now so you can release that cloud which encompasses you.

Friends, we are gathered here today to celebrate a departed relationship. As in all relationships there were ups and downs, struggles and triumphs, exhilaration and disappointment. We are here to focus on the positives, the wisdom garnered.

I am grateful that my marriage taught me how to:

💜 *Negotiate win/win solutions.*

💜 *Not worry about inconsequential disagreements.*

💜 *Get clear on what was important to discuss and what wasn't.*

💜 *Give positive reinforcement.*

💜 *Live with not always getting my way.*

💜 *Go out of my way to give my mate what would please him.*

💜 *Not use my knowledge of his emotional buttons to manipulate him.*

💜 *Have patience with him when he didn't do well what came easily for me.*

💜 *Be "in wonder" when he did something that seemed inconceivable to me (in the* Dipping Your Toe in the Dating Pool: Dive In Without Belly Flopping *book).*

💜 *Love deeply.*

💜 *Laugh at myself.*

💜 *Appreciate things that were important to him.*

💜 *Be trusting and vulnerable.*

💜 *Forgive him when he did things that I found insensitive or objectionable.*

💜 *Deal with disappointments.*

♥ *Be monogamous.*

♥ *Keep the passion alive.*

So while this marriage has passed, it left behind valued skills which will live on in the next relationship.

News flash: Man goes poof

An Adventures in Delicious Dating After 40 reader wrote:

> *I was dating a man, then he quit his job of twenty years and seemed overwhelmed with stuff in his life. However, he kept assuring me we were fine. For months we talked every day — we knew exactly when to get a hold of each other. We had no secrets. I could even be at his place when he wasn't there. We had many overnights, and talked frequently, confiding very personal stuff.*
>
> *Then something shifted. I went to his place, he was home, but avoided me. Then some weird messages, telling me about silly little things. Then nothing for over 2 months. I believe he became depressed. He is over 50, very professional, and all signs indicate he would be completely forthright with any need to split with me.*
>
> *My conundrum is, do I assume — and there are*

many indications — that he is depressed and I emotionally support him? Or do I act like I normally would when someone disappears and just move on?

I've asked him to tell me if I should stop contacting him. I made it very clear that I only need to be told once. Then, on the other hand, I'm willing to stick by if it's a health issue.

What are your thoughts?

This is a toughy. You have a good history with him, so you don't want to assume the worst. It sounds like you haven't actually talked to him. I would call or set a time for coffee or go to his house (or he yours). If he is depressed, it would be hard for him to reach out. Extending your hand of support could be just what he needs to seek professional help and get his life back on track.

Or perhaps he got back with an old love or started seeing someone else but didn't know how to break it to you. His avoiding behavior then nothing could be interpreted that way, but you won't really know until you ask.

If he doesn't return your phone calls, don't leave him angry messages, just be supportive. Assume that your analysis is in some part right and leave the door open for him to reach out. But don't wait on him, date others. You've already waited for him two months, so if you haven't already, see others. If he comes back around and you aren't attached to another, you can see him again. Or perhaps just shift to friend mode.

When breaking up is taking a stand

You've stayed with him because it is magical when you are with him. He treats you like a queen. You have interesting conversations. He makes you laugh. And when you touch — electricity. You know this combination is rare, so you've put up with the parts that aren't great.

But your needs aren't being met. You've shared with him several times the specifics of what you need in a relationship. You know he heard you as he's repeated them back to you and you occasionally see attempts at his giving you what you want. But there's not consistent effort. So you feel frustrated at not getting what is important to you.

You've talked to him about it and he promises to do better. Which he does for a day or so. He doesn't seem to be willing or able to consistently give you what you need, even though your needs seem pretty basic to you. How onerous is connecting daily, seeing each other at least once a week, making plans to see each other at least a day in advance? For him, apparently, Herculean.

You've given him 95% of what he says he needs, and told him you are uncomfortable with the remaining 5%, which he said he's willing to live with. You asked if he has any yet unspoken needs. He said no.

You decide you need to release this man, although giving up the yummy parts is hard. But you know if you continue to see him, you won't experience someone who consistently shows he wants to make you happy, just as you want to make your partner happy.

Giving up the yummy parts is hard

You are taking a stand. Not only for how you want to be treated, but for your future with a man who understands you and clearly wants to be with you.

For some women it is hard to take a stand — to say, "This isn't working for me." Then to take action to remedy the situation. Sometimes the act of taking a stand will help him see that he needs to do something dramatic if he wants to be in your life. Or perhaps he will agree that it isn't working for him, either. And you'll both make adjustments or decide to part ways.

If you've given concerted effort to express your needs, and he doesn't say he can provide them or seems uninterested in helping you get your needs met, then it isn't a match. Unless he said he would absolutely give you what you said you need then doesn't, there's no need to be angry. It's just a mismatch. And the earlier you see that and extricate yourself, the happier both of you will be.

I've struggled with this myself, as the good times can overshadow what's missing. So I delude myself that it's working and stay in the relationship longer than I should. Often it is he who pulls the plug and while it can hurt, after that pain has subsided, it is easier to see it is really for the best. And in an odd way I'm grateful he had the courage to do something that I was unable to do — at least at the time.

Paranoid or observant?

You've been dating around for a few years, having second dates or more with a dozen or so men. You have enough experience under your belt to notice that in the past there's been a shift of behavior that has preceded a guy's going poof or breaking up with you. There's a change in something that he had done predictably. Maybe he usually makes contact at least once a day, or typically asks you out for the weekend by Thursday, or wants to have lunch during the week as well as Saturday night.

Because of the behaviors of past guys, you're on the lookout with the man you've been seeing for a few months. You've been blindsided in the past, but in retrospect the signs of a change were there, you just didn't interpret them as pre-break-up or pre-poof signals.

You're watching for a shift in pattern that might reveal a change in his perspective about you. You are aware if he skips a day of contact, since he typically calls/IMs/texts each day. You contact him on those days, and he seems glad to hear from you (assuming you don't yell at or guilt him). You try to not be overly sensitive, bordering on paranoid. But you notice when there's a change in patterns.

You wrestle with yourself to not make more out of it than that he was really busy or distracted by work/kids/ life. But the question resurfaces,"Is this the beginning of the end?"

Ideally, you let it be, noticing but not commenting unless it happens a handful of times. At times life gets overwhelming for most people, and as long as a missed day of contact doesn't spread into three or four days, you're probably fine. However, if the pattern of pulling away begins to repeat itself, don't be surprised if he goes poof or you get one of those dreaded "it's not working" emails.

Even if you bring it up as gently as pos- sible, with no blame or guilt, it's a rare man who will admit he's having second thoughts about your seeing each other. Some will try to cover it up, more from not wanting to hurt you or have a confrontation than from purposefully lying. This doesn't mean you shouldn't bring it up — you should see what he says. But even if he comes back with, "I've just been crazy busy with work and the kids lately" he will know that you've no- ticed and it may help him feel okay about coming clean. It's like when as a kid your mom found you doing some- thing you shouldn't have, at first you may fib to see if

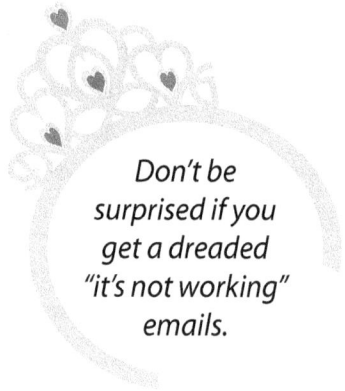

> *Don't be surprised if you get a dreaded "it's not working" emails.*

she will ignore it. But if you had any conscience and your mother was not crazy, you may have confessed to her after a while.

And this knife cuts both ways. If you find yourself behaving differently toward him than in the past, perhaps your feelings have changed and you just haven't articulated them yet. If you used to answer no matter when he called, and now you let it go to voice mail if you're doing something else that may be a sign you're less engaged. Or you used to invite him to dinner during the week and now you'd rather watch "The Bachelor," notice if you're feeling less interested in your time with him.

So notice the shifts and see if they are signs you should pay attention to or just ignore. If you choose the latter, at least you won't be completely blindsided when the "Have a nice life" email comes through.

You learn a lot about a man by how he breaks up

A man discloses volumes during a dating relationship, but most revealing is how he breaks up. It's almost a shame that there isn't a break up early on as you'd see how he treats you.

If a man breaks up via text, IM, or email, I know he's a coward, afraid to have a mature discussion about his feelings and the relationship. Most of the men who've broken up with me have done it this way or by just going poof, not contacting me again, nor returning my attempts to find out what's going on.

In a recent text breakup message, my now ex-beau refused to elaborate or explain what was going on with him. Previously when he'd expressed some unfulfilled — and heretofore unexpressed — needs, by talking it out we came up with a mutually satisfactory solution.

But this time he treated me like one of his children: his decision was final and he wasn't discussing it, even to help me understand, not dissuade him. How respected I felt — not!

Rarely has a man sat me down and discussed his feelings and desire to discontinue our romantic relationship. I've actually grown more fond of the few men who've done this and respected their willingness to initiate tough conversations. Typically we've remained friends afterward.

If a relationship is difficult, volatile, turbulent or one of the parties is cantankerous or abusive, best to break up virtually. But only one of mine has been that way. In fact, some breakups have come on the heels of his telling me how much he cared about me, adored me, and/or thought we were a perfect match. So then to have a man break up without further explanation leaves me with a lot of head scratching.

It is best to remind yourself that a man who breaks up this way shows his disrespect for you and his incapacity to maturely discuss difficult topics, so no matter how much you cared for him, it is best to let him drift back into the dating pool. He obviously hasn't learned how to swim in your waters, so let him go back to the turbulent whirlpool he's doomed to spin in until — and if — he learns how to behave maturely and respectfully.

Closure is a good thing

received an IM from my most recent ex-beau apologizing for having hurt and disappointed me. It allowed me to have closure, even though I had already released him in my mind and moved on. But actual closure, if done sanely, maturely and with care, has value even though closure just in your mind can be satisfying.

In our 45-minute discussion I was able to tell him how deeply he hurt me and share my feelings. I had considered doing this via email but thought he might delete it without opening it. So the IM discussion gave me the opportunity to share with him my reaction to his insensitive text and I know he heard me, whether or not he fully understood how his actions affected me.

> *It allowed me to have closure*

While he didn't seem contrite about how or what he said in his breakup text, he did acknowledge what I shared and apologized throughout for causing me anguish. But he also reiterated his decision. This was not an "I'm sorry, please forgive me, take me back" discussion. Both of us acknowledged the love and kindness the other had shown us, but that we now saw some critical ingredients were missing. We wished each other the best of luck in finding someone to meet our needs.

Although IMing this kind of conversation seems cold, it actually was easier for me as I was able to think through what I wanted to say in my message. Also, I would have had a hard time talking through the tears, but typing was not a problem.

It felt good to express my feelings and know they were received. This kind of closure feels much more complete than the one-sided closures we make in our mind when a man refuses to discuss his decision to move on or just goes poof.

Rejection is protection

In response to a friend asking how I was doing, I told him of my most recent breakup experience — how cavalierly and insensitively my now-ex beau communicated his decision. I told my friend that despite my focusing on all the ways this man treated me disrespectfully, I was having a heck of a time moving on.

My wise friend responded, "Often rejection is protection. Think about how his personality would have shown up later on, with even more dire consequences." My friend was right. If this guy could so coldly abandon our connection after his numerous expressions of devotion and adoration, what if my blind love had allowed us to continue? I'd have even more emotion and time investment in a man who wasn't right for me.

When you are reeling from it, rejection does not look like a blessing

When you are reeling from it, rejection does not look like a blessing. But even if the rejection isn't heartbreaking, it is a clear sign that something is not right. To pretend otherwise is to live in a fantasyland. A place I find myself residing a bit too often.

So rejection — even if a cordial "thanks, but no thanks," is protecting your heart from something that isn't a fit. I think I'm getting closer to just saying, "Thank you" and moving on without anguish.

How women sabotage potential relationships

Both parties in a budding relationship can sabotage it without knowing it. Whether it's myriad small things or one deal breaker, these acts can make the other disengage and we may not even know what happened.

A pal shared an example of how a woman with whom he was beginning to have a relationship sabotaged his connection to her.

He said:

Seven years ago, I became friends with a woman at work who told me of her failed marriage. She'd followed a man overseas, and then after he went on a 3-month assignment abroad without her, he said he wanted a divorce.

Returning to the states, she soon hooked up with a guy, followed him to another state, and gave up her dreams for him. She stayed in this emotionally abusive relationship for 5 years with man with a mental disorder and drug problem.

Throughout this we emailed sporadically. After the dysfunctional relationship ended, I told her I'd been attracted to her for a while. She said she could fall for me — I was everything she wanted. It scared her.

She sabotaged the budding potentially great relationship

She sabotaged the budding potentially great relationship at least five times:

💜 *After canceling twice, she made a plan to come to my state to see me. She cancelled again. Flakiness — strike one.*

💜 *She told me, "You probably think I'm a bad person and a bad friend for cancelling." Strike 2: Too self-deprecating showing low self-esteem and projecting what she thinks I think.*

💜 *She visited the next month saying she would stay with relatives. She ends up spending the night with me but we don't have sex. Upon returning home, she texts and calls saying "I miss you so much." We have a discussion which turns into a disagreement. She later says it was her fault for projecting her anxieties on me. Strike 3: A bit too psy-*

choanalyzing.

💜 *Before departing for a vacation, she said she wanted to see me so books the departure and return from my airport. She'll see me on the way out and on the way back. Three days before her departure we have another discussion about the future. She says her life is too busy and concludes we are not compatible. She decides it's better she not see me before and after her trip. She decided to come to see me for a few hours before her flight. I took her to the airport. When she returned, I picked her up and she spent the night with me. Strike 4: She can't decide what she wants and waffles.*

💜 *After returning home, she said she was too busy to see me for the next month. She thinks we should take it more slowly but she doesn't think it's possible for me to do so. Strike 5: She's projecting something without checking it out with me, as that was not how I felt.*

There were other ways she sabotaged the relationship before it got very far. I quickly saw that she had too many issues that negated my attraction to her, so I stopped contacting her.

We could argue that some of what he counted as sabotage wouldn't be for us. But the point is they appeared that way to him. We could be amazed he hung in as long as he did, but I've put up with more than five acts that sabotaged a relationship and still kept seeing the guy. The important point is that we can be doing things that are sabotaging our own relationships and have no idea we're doing it. So we can't stop it in future relationships.

Since it is unlikely a man will articulate our acts that undermine the relationship, we can only learn what our man considers relationship spoilers. So ask the man you're dating what past women have done that turned him off. Then see if you do any of those are behaviors.

Uneven ardor

It's wonderful when dating someone who has the same level of infatuation you do. It's fabulous to both feel similarly smitten.

However, my experience is it isn't that common to feel equal adoration. One of you is typically more entranced than the other.

It isn't that common to feel equal adoration.

When it's you who's head-over-heels and he's not feeling it to the same degree, you can feel embarrassed at your infatuation. You tend to be the one who initiates conversations and encounters, or at least the overtures are weighted to your side. You hear yourself asking him, "When will I see you again," although you know that sounds clingy and needy — you can't seem to help yourself.

If he's the one who's beguiled, you can still be embarrassed. His frequent calls to say he's thinking of you, his flow of emails, IMs or texts telling you how beauti-

ful, wonderful, and/or sexy you are can be overwhelming, even if they don't reach stalker velocity. His show-
ering you with flowers or gifts is touching and sweet,
but when you know you don't feel similarly, they can be
hard to accept.

I once dated a man for 3 months who wanted us
to move in together. Because of distance, we only saw
each other a few days every two weeks. I felt I barely
knew him, although we talked and emailed often in between assignations. He would bring or send me a small
gift every week. Even when I was traveling, he'd have
something delivered to my room. I was fond of him, yet
not in love. Finally, I had to pull the plug as I saw it was
unfair to him to keep accepting his affection and gifts
when I was not feeling myself falling for him and did
not honestly feel I would.

Doing what's right, not what's easy

At dinner with 3 other midlife dating women, one asked for input on a situation.

She'd gone out with a man three times. While she said she enjoyed his company, she didn't feel any romantic attraction. He'd asked her to call him when she returned from a recent trip, which she had that day.

She didn't want to call him. She said, "What would I say? That I didn't want to go out with him again? That seems dumb and hurtful. If I don't call him, won't he get the message?"

> *She didn't want to call him.*

We all agreed that the easy way out was not to call him. But the easy way was not the right way.

All of us had experienced men going poof and none of us liked it. Especially if we'd gone out with someone several times. We all felt it was disrespectful.

Her not calling him is not only disrespecting him, it is, in fact, disrespecting her. Anytime we don't act the way we know is "right," we ignore our own moral compass. I said that I wanted to behave in a way that had me respect my own actions, even when they involved something that was uncomfortable or difficult.

I think we all want to respect ourselves and feel we are acting with character. The dictionary defines that as "The mental and moral qualities distinctive to an individual; a person's good reputation." Many of us have been told that character is doing what is right when no one is looking.

We need to have character in dating, whether we call it that or integrity, backbone, uprightness, moral strength, or something else. We get frustrated when the men we date don't personify these traits. But that doesn't mean we don't need to — for our own self-respect.

When broken trust is irreparable

Solid relationships are built on trust. So what happens when one of the pair does something that strains — or completely breaks — that trust?

If it's a one-time, never-to-be-repeated event, and the bond is strong, often the offending party receives grace and forgiveness and the relationship continues.

But what if there are multiple fibs, lies or less-than-forthcoming responses to direct questions? What if someone chooses to keep certain facts to themselves to keep their options open?

A friend shared that early in the relationship, a now ex-girlfriend had fibbed to him on several occasions. The most egregious was when she announced her ex-boyfriend was coming to visit her. My friend asked where he'd be staying. With her, she said matter-of-factly. Not feeling completely comfortable with this arrangement, he probed deeper hoping to quell any doubts he had. Knowing she didn't have a guest room in her small apartment, he asked, "And where will he be sleeping?" "I don't know. We haven't discussed it. Last time we shared my bed." "Did you have sex?" "No."

Knowing how amorous she was, he said he didn't feel comfortable with this arrangement. She asked the ex-beau to sleep on her couch.

Later she admitted that the last time they'd shared a bed they indeed did have sex. She lied, she explained, as she didn't want my friend to be concerned. I think she didn't want to lose him and thought that information might have driven him away. She wanted to keep her options open.

She wanted to keep her options open.

They broke up six months later over other issues yet kept in contact. A few weeks later, she accepted his dinner and movie invitation. They held hands, cuddled and seemed like they were back together. She neglected to share that she had a new boyfriend with whom she was already sleeping. She wanted to see if it might work out with my friend — she wanted to keep her options open. She held all her cards close and didn't want to put any on the table.

It would have been more mature if before accepting the dinner invitation to say, "I really like you and understand why we broke up. I'd love to see you and discuss if we might be able to sort out our differences.

And I need to let you know I've started seeing someone and we've become close. I want you to know what's happening with me so we can talk openly and candidly." That would have allowed my friend to make decisions that were right for him based all the information — not just the information she wanted to share.

Have we all been duplicitous at times? I'm guessing yes. I know I have. But now as I've gotten older and hopefully wiser, I see how disrespectful, controlling and selfish it is to withhold information that the other really should know. If I was on the other side and would want to know it I am now better at sharing it. It is usually not easy to say, yet if you take your time to share the information with care and compassion, it will be easier to discuss. I have been sincerely thanked after sharing something I knew the other didn't want to hear, and have thanked others for telling me things that stung at first.

Trust is built by keeping your word, acting congruent with your words, being willing to discuss difficult topics without upset, and consistent action that shows you care about the other person as well as yourself. When trust is strained or broken early in a relationship, it's nearly impossible to repair.

Haunting exes

Y ou glimpse a man who looks strikingly like a past love.

In front of you at Starbucks stands a guy wearing your former sweetie's cologne.

The song plays on the radio that you slow-danced to with your ex, naked in front of the fire on New Year's Eve.

Snippet reminders of a past beau waft into your life. You're transported to a special time with a special man. You linger a moment, smiling, before remembering why you are no longer together.

These memories are apparitions of lingering love.

These memories are apparitions of lingering love. They represent a wonderful feeling of when you were in love and felt love in return.

Depending on where your mind drifts after that glimmer, you will either enjoy these reminders or despise them.

If you use them to jog feelings of love, and know it's possible to have that warmth again, you see these as omens of what's ahead for you.

If you are drawn into memories of disrespect, fights, infidelity, or worse, you will curse these emotional triggers. If they cause you sadness because a special person isn't in your life now, or a longing to reunite with an abusive or unfit partner, then you need to stop that thinking and turn it into thoughts that serve you.

It's not easy to control our thoughts, especially when emotional triggers cause us to be "out of our mind," even momentarily. Yet we must control our reactions to these triggers and choose to dwell on thoughts that help us rather than detract from what we want.

You can use haunting thoughts of your ex to hold you back or propel you forward. It's your choice.

How have you framed recurring triggers from exes — as positive signs or negative?

Move forward or move on

A question from a reader:

> *"I've been seeing a guy for 6 months and we still*
> *can't get farther than a quick peck on the lips or a*
> *quick impersonal hug. I've told him I want more*
> *intimacy but still nothing. What should I do?"*

Many men say it's up to the woman to set the pace of physical involvement and they don't want to overstep their bounds. They have learned to be respectful of a woman's boundaries and don't want to press those without explicit permission.

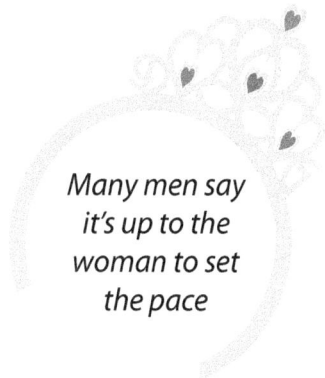

Many men say it's up to the woman to set the pace

He might have been chastised in the past from a woman who took offense at his moving things forward more quickly than she liked. Or even though you stated you were ready, he may not be.

After dating exclusively for three months and physically progressing up to a point, I once asked a beau, "What do you need to feel comfortable having sex together?" He said he needed to feel in love with me. We then discussed that while we were both very fond of each other, neither of us was in love. A few weeks later we discussed how we'd given it 3.5 months and wasn't happening for either of us, so we decided to shift to being friends. Now he's a treasured pal.

So you could ask, "What do you need to feel comfortable moving our relationship forward?" Or you could just pull him back to you the next time he pecks you and go in for a more involved kiss — and see what he does!

The point being something has to shift. You want to either progress or move the relationship to friendship.

Taking the hard way out

W hen you've decided you don't want further contact with someone, it's easy to ignore their phone calls, IMs, texts or emails.

Perhaps you rise a level to at least send a "we're not a match" email.

It's hardest to actually tell the person face-to-face. However, if you've only had one encounter, it seems counter-productive to arrange a meeting just to tell the person you won't be seeing them again.

So a phone call is in order. But what do you say? How do you phrase it to not focus on the other's deal breakers? You don't want to stoop to a level of name calling or pointing out the other's bad breath, disheveled appearance, incessant cursing, bad manners or lusting after you. You want to do this task with class and leave the other's dignity intact.

You procrastinate making the call because you don't want an altercation and since you barely know the person, you have no idea how he'll respond.

But you decide you must act consistent with how you'd like to be treated — respectfully — so you make the call.

This was the thought process I recently went through to decide how to tell Erotic-Dream-Guy he shouldn't bother contacting me again. He'd called 4 times in the previous 3 days and I didn't pick up because I was busy at the time. But I also didn't call him back.

I thought about our interactions and how I felt during and afterward. While he was funny, smart and knew many of the right things to say, he also chastised me for telling my truth, told me I was evasive when I thought I was being polite, and had made many blatant sexual remarks even after I told him I was uncomfortable with them. Generally, I felt disrespected which is intolerable for me.

So I dialed. I thought about what I would say and how to phrase it to be as non-blaming as possible. I didn't want to lie with the common, "I'm taking a break from dating," or "I've met someone else and we really hit it off." Neither were true, and I'd heard these so often I know they are avoidance lines.

I didn't want to lie.

He answered and asked about my weekend. I told him it had been busy (which it had) and I knew he'd called a number of times. He said he'd like to see me again. I thanked him and continued, "Because you are a direct man, I'll be direct with you. After our last conversation I determined that we want different things and we weren't a match." He said he was disappointed and respected my decision. He didn't ask for clarification, so I didn't elaborate. I thanked him for his interest and wished him good luck. He said thank you and we hung up.

If he'd become confrontational and said, "What do you mean we want different things" I was prepared with a comment that I know is nasty: "I want a respectful gentleman. You want to get laid." Luckily, I didn't have to stoop to this low-level comment. I don't like myself when I become snarky.

It is much harder to tell someone personally, not in text, IM or email, that you don't want further contact, but it is, I believe, the right way. Have I always made the effort? No. But I felt cowardly when I took the easy way out. Dating is hard enough when you have to deal with cowardly people along the way. I think we need to have the courage to do what we know is right and treat others respectfully, even when they have not always behaved that way toward you. Their bad behavior is no excuse for you to lower yourself to their level.

Breakup a time to

reassess

A midlife friend recently broke up with his girlfriend of 10 years. The reason he broke up with her is after a lot of soul searching and couples counseling, it became clear they wanted different things.

When I asked how he was doing regarding this, he said he was using this as an impetus to reassess many things in his life.

The was using this as an impetus to reassess many things in his life.

"Like what?" I asked.

"Pretty much every-thing."

"Give me some ex-amples."

"Work, living situation, exercise, diet, goals, love, relationships. I'm stepping back and looking at most elements of my life and asking if they are what I want. Am

I doing my the best I can given certain parameters?"

"Wow, that's a lot to assess."

"Yes, it's good."

Breakups can be a time to examine many elements of your life and decide if each is what you want. As a result of this assessment, many people increase their exercise, change their diet, go back to school, take up new hobbies, modify their appearance and/or wardrobe, negotiate work duties, remodel their house or even move.

When my marriage dissolved I thought hard about if I wanted to continue living in my house and city. I seriously pondered getting in my car and visiting friends around the country who'd invited me. I could then experience many areas for possible relocation. Funds and lethargy prevented me from taking off on this adventure. But since I've visited so many areas of the country, I decided I was happy for now where I am.

After my last painful breakup, I was motivated to seek counseling to better understand the bad choices I was making about men. It has helped immensely.

What have you examined and changed after a breakup? Have breakups motivated you to modify important parts of your life?

Full-court press

While most women appreciate attention and a man expressing his interest, sometimes there can be too much too soon. Then it feels smothering or borderline stalking.

This week a new man contacted me from a dating site. He met the minimum requirements and seemed interesting, although he's geographically undesirable. But I was intrigued enough to respond.

Quickly he sent me a long missive detailing more of his life than I really needed or cared to know at this point. He asked questions, some of which I choose not to answer because it would have taken too long to type. He offered his phone number and said he'd gladly call me if I preferred.

The next day I responded with my number, telling him I was traveling and would be available after 8 p.m. the next day. So imagine my surprise when he called the same day during a layover between flights. I had things to do during this time, so I was a little annoyed he didn't wait until I'd said I'd be available, nor did he ask if this was a good time to chat.

I was polite, but quickly excused myself telling him I had to get some things done in the terminal before my next flight.

He gave me the link to his Internet sports radio show and asked me to listen to a few of the previous shows. I listened to one, and was put off by his profanity and anger-laced commentary.

When I got home, I was exhausted and went to bed. He called and woke me up. I let it go to voice mail. When I listened to it the next day, he said he'd hoped I'd gotten home safely.

When I checked my email, there was a press release from him ranting about some current sports issue. I skimmed the release and saw it had the same angry tone as his radio show. While I appreciate passion for one's work, when that crosses the line into anger, it's unappealing.

This man seems needy and desperate. I'm not interested in getting involved with someone with anger issues and no healthy sense of appropriateness or boundaries. This one will have to shower his attention on someone with more patience or interest.

Have you had someone put a full-court press on you? How did you let him know it was too much too fast?

Resources

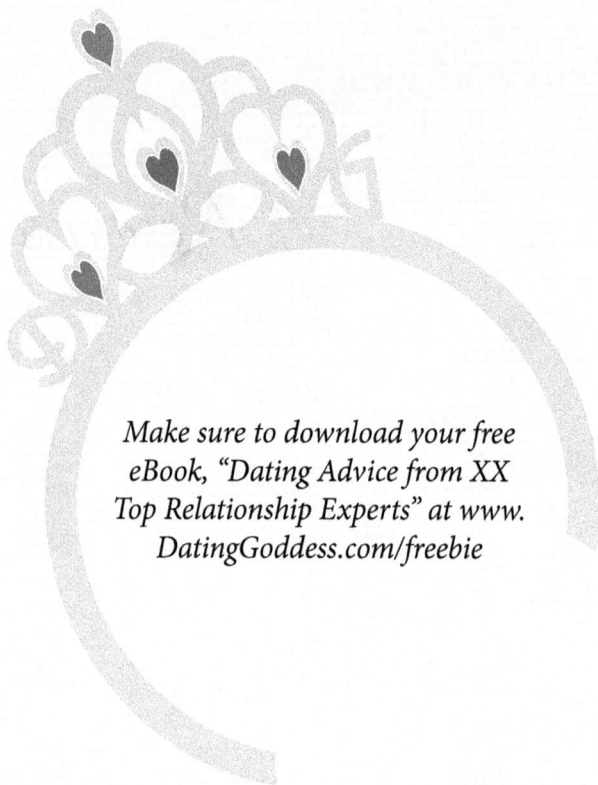

Make sure to download your free eBook, "Dating Advice from XX Top Relationship Experts" at www. DatingGoddess.com/freebie

Afterword

At the time of this writing, I have not yet found my true King Charming. I continue my search with verve. I've become more discerning about what I want and don't want. I've met some wonderful men pals — my treasures — who continue to be in touch.

I wish you much luck in your adventure. It will be fun and frustrating, exhilarating and exasperating, and sexy or sexless. So much depends on you, your approach and your attitude. My books are designed to help you enjoy as much as possible and ward off unpleasantness. But nearly all adventures have wonderful highs as well as a few lows. If you know that going in and arm yourself with information on what to expect, you'll have more of the positives and fewer of the negatives.

Please drop by www.DatingGoddess.com and join in the discussion and report on your experiences.

Dating Goddess

Resources

o to www.datinggoddess.com to access a variety of useful resources. We work to suggest resources we think have value.

Dating and relationship book reviews

These reviews will save you time and money as I've given you my take on specific books, CDs and more. Some are worth your effort to buy and read or listen to them — some are not. We're always adding new book reviews, so check frequently. We'll also notify our mailing list when new resources are added.

Dating site links

There are a lot of dating sites on the Internet. I've listed the ones I think are worth investigating.

Dating products and tools

Dating can be daunting. We're continually looking at

ways to make it easier and more fun. We'll provide info on games, tools, even date-wear that will help others know you're available, or help you get to know potential suitors better.

Dating and relationship advice sites

Advice "experts" abound on the Internet as any-one can self-proclaim themseves as expert — even if they haven't dated in 30 years and never in midlife. I've worked to find experts who's advice I generally think is solid.

Midlife recources

We'll feature Web sites, books, events and other re-sources we think might interest you.

Newly discovered resources

I'll add other resources as we discover them, sub-scribe to our mailing list to get the scoop as soon as we find them. Go to www.DatingGoddess.com to register for our mailing list. Don't worry, we won't sell or give your email to anyone.

Acknowledgments

Let me start by acknowledging the 112 men who helped trigger the lessons contained in this book. Some prompted several! They remain nameless here to protect their identity, although most would recognize references to them. Plus the thousands more whose winks, emails and calls didn't result in a date, but helped me learn the dating game. And all those men who I emailed who never responded — such a blessing to have them weed themselves out.

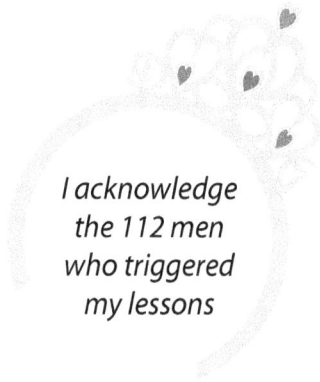

I acknowledge the 112 men who triggered my lessons

I'd like to thank my Seven Sisters mastermind group for the tremendous brainstorming, noodling, strategizing and encouragement. I wouldn't have begun this project without the prodding of Val Cade, Chris Clarke-Epstein, Mariah Burton Nelson, Sue Dyer, Sam Horn and Marilynn Mobley.

Thank you to my good friends who've listened to my dating stories ad nauseam, and whose support and wisdom are embedded in this text. Ed Betts, Ken Braly, Bruce Daley, Tom Drews, Elaine Floyd, Paulette Ensign, Scott Friedman, Craig Harrison, Mary Jansen, Tom Johnson, Sandy Jones, Mary Kilkenny, Ellie Klevins, Patrick Lynch, Mary Marcdante, Barbara McNichol, Ann Peterson, Anthony Ramsey, Caterina Rando, Kristy Rogers, Jana Stanfield, Holly Steil, Terry Tepliz, and George Walther, thank you.

The Adventures in Delicious Dating After 40 series

The *Adventures in Delicious Dating After 40* series is designed to help you understand your own midlife dating journey. It is not a road map, as we all take different routes. It is a guide to help you understand yourself, midlife men, and the dating process. Hopefully, you'll not only learn from the lessons and insights shared in this series, but you'll examine how they apply — or don't — to your own dating adventure.

You'll get the scoop on what you need to know, what's changed since you last dated, and how to navigate inevitable bumps in the road.

Following is an overview of each book in the series and a sampling of some of the chapter titles. All are detailed at www.DatingGoddess.com.

Date or Wait: Are You Ready for Mr. Great?

Are you ready for a special man in your life? You have a great life. But you know you'd like a special man to share it. You think you're ready to date, but you haven't done it in a while.

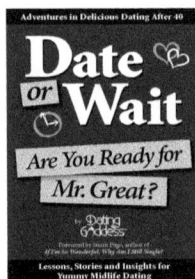

What should you consider before you actually start dating full bore? Even if you've reentered the dating world, this will give you a foundation of attitude and philosophy to make your adventure more fulfilling.

Sample chapters

💜 From hurt to flirt

💜 Dating is like Baskin-Robbins

💜 You've got to kiss a lot of…princes!

💜 What's your definition of dating success?

💜 Are you open to receiving?

💜 Dating: A self-designed personal-growth workshop

💜 Hands-on dating research

💜 Being present to the presents

💜 Being aggressively single

💜 Approaching dating like a buffet

💜 Is Brad Pitt ruining your love life?

💜 Treasures can come in dented packages

Assessing Your Assets: Why You're A Great Catch

You have many wonderful qualities. But it's easy to focus on one's flaws — at least what seem like flaws to you. However, to the right man your imperfections are endearing, attractive and lovable. You have to be clear what you offer a man who will find you enchanting.

Assessing Your Assets helps you look at what you bring to a new relationship. It will help you see your good points so you'll approach dating with more confidence.

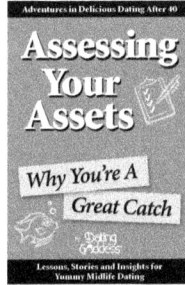

Sample chapters

🖤 Don't think you are damaged goods

🖤 You are (probably) more attractive than you think!

🖤 They aren't called "hate handles"

🖤 Are you a good man picker?

🖤 What are your deal breakers?

🖤 Are you arguing your limitations?

🖤 Turn your liabilities into assets

🖤 The strong vs. nice woman debate

🖤 Is your sense of humor stunting your dating?

🖤 Why are we drawn to bad boys?

🖤 The zest test

In Search of King Charming: Who Do I Want to Share My Throne?

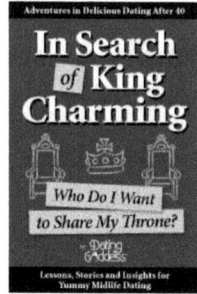

You are no longer looking for "Prince" Charming because you are a queen. You want someone who is at your level, not groveling at your feet. You want a king — someone who's your equal and with whom you can rule the throne together!

This book focuses on helping you better define what you want beyond tall, dark and handsome! You'll consider characteristics you might not have thought of before. You'll look at what you want now.

Sample chapters

💜 Building your Franken-boyfriend

💜 What's your "perfect boyfriend's" job description?

💜 A man to go with your wardrobe

💜 In search of the elusive good kisser

💜 When you're clear on what you want, it appears

💜 Are you dating the same guy in different bodies?

💜 Does he fit in your world?

💜 What's your kissing quotient?

💜 Is your guy's loving muscle strong?

💜 Do you both have the same dating rhythm?

Embracing Midlife Men:
Insights Into Curious Behaviors

Do you sometimes scratch your head after interacting with a midlife man, wondering, "What could he possibly be thinking?" Especially if it's before, during or after a date with a man who presumably wants to impress you!

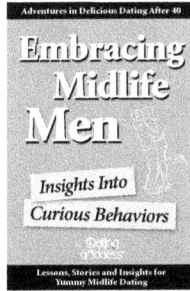

This book focuses on better understanding midlife men's behaviors. When you grasp what's going on in his head it's much easier to embrace him. Men are wondrous creatures, so we need to understand them better and love them for who they are.

Sample chapters

💜 Men are like shoes

💜 Why men disappear when it gets serious

💜 Chivalry isn't dead —but it seems to be hibernating

💜 Do men want feisty women?

💜 Midlife men have forgotten how to date

💜 Are you getting prime time from your man?

💜 When a man tells you what he paid for things

💜 Does he treat you like his ex?

💜 Has Greg Behrendt done women a disservice?

💜 Tales of woo

Dipping Your Toe in the Dating Pool: Dive In Without Belly Flopping

You've decided you are ready — you want to start dating. Maybe you've already had a few coffee dates with several men. You want to be as successful as possible on your dating adventure.

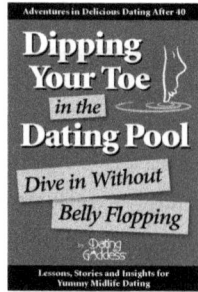

This book focuses on getting started on your dating adventures. We cover what you need to know as you begin your journey.

Sample chapters

♥ Do you have the right datewear?

♥ Dating with integrity

♥ Building your rejection muscle

♥ When "be yourself" is questionable advice

♥ Faux beaus and practice dating

♥ Are you making bad decisions out of loneliness?

♥ Being "in wonder" about your date's behavior

♥ When do you feel most vulnerable in dating?

♥ Are you out of his league — or he yours?

♥ Why listening is so seductive

Winning at the Online Dating Game: Stack the Deck in Your Favor

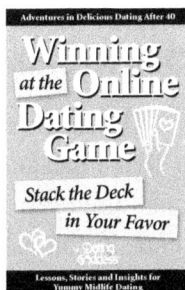

Internet dating can be frustrating or fruitful. It will be much less exasperating if you know how to read and weed out men's profiles that aren't appropriate for you. And you'll have a steady stream of potential suitors if you know how to write a compelling profile for yourself.

This book focuses on the ins and outs of online dating. How to play the game, which has it's own rules and language. If you don't understand how online dating works, you'll waste a lot of time connecting with men who are not a possible fit for you.

Sample chapters

💜 Shopping for men

💜 Safe online dating

💜 Is 21st Century dating unnatural?

💜 What do men look at in your profile?

💜 Euphemisms uncovered

💜 Are you describing yourself compellingly?

💜 No, I will not be dating your Harley

💜 Playing the online dating game

💜 Scantily clothed pictures

Check Him Out Before Going Out: Avoiding Dud Dates

Under the cloak of the anonymity that email and the phone provides, men often reveal more than they intend. If you ask the right questions you can find out a lot about his values and view of the world after just an interaction or two.

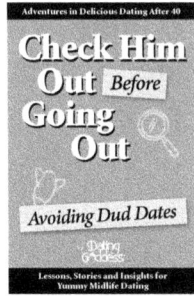

This book focuses on what you need to ask before agreeing to even a coffee date. You need to vet the men who email and call you to ensure you're not likely to waste your time with men who clearly aren't a match.

Sample chapters

💜 Becoming smitten with the fantasy

💜 Can Google help — or hinder — your dating life?

💜 Qualify your potential dates before meeting

💜 The art of consideration

💜 Anticipating a big date is like awaiting Santa

💜 Being seduced by what he is over who he is

💜 Are you his spare?

💜 My boyfriend, whom I haven't met

💜 When canceling is the right thing to do

💜 Politics, religion and sex — oh my!

First-Rate First Dates: Increasing the Chances of a Second Date

You can tell a lot about someone within the first 30 minutes. What does he talk about? Does he ask you questions? If so, what does he want to know about you? What do you need to know about him? How does he treat you? How does he treat those around you?

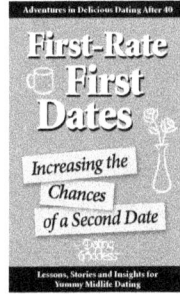

This book focuses on what goes on during the first date. How do you determine if you want a second date? What you can do to increase the likelihood your date will ask you for a second? That is if you want a repeat!

Sample chapters

💜 Start with coffee

💜 How do you greet him?

💜 When it clicks, throw out some of your criteria

💜 Tracking your date's score

💜 Clues a guy is just looking for a booty call

💜 12 signs he won't be asking for a second date

💜 First-date red flags that this guy isn't for you

💜 Honesty is not always the best policy

💜 Chemistry, or does he make my toes curl?

💜 Women's first-date blunders

Real Deal or Faux Beau: Should You Keep Seeing Him?

You've begun to go out with a man you like. How do you decide if you should continue seeing him, or if you should release him because he's not The One?

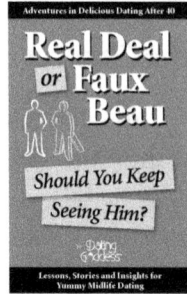

This book focuses on second dates and beyond. During the dating process you are both assessing if you want to keep seeing each other. This book helps you determine what questions you need to ask yourself.

Sample chapters

💜 Deciding to see him again or not

💜 What's your date's Delight/Disappointment Scale score?

💜 Broaching tough conversations

💜 "I want to respect me in the morning"

💜 Does he invite you to his place?

💜 Are you stingy in dating?

💜 When his hand is on your knee too soon

💜 Easy way to ask hard questions

💜 Rose-colored glasses obscure red flags

💜 If his stories don't add up, subtract yourself

Multidating Responsibly: Play the Field Without Being A Player

Playing the field is frowned on in some circles. There are definitely appropriate and inappropriate ways to date several men simultaneously.

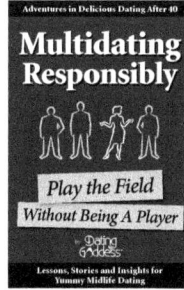

This book focuses on how to date around responsibly and with integrity without leading men on. If you do it with honesty, you can date several people at once until you're both ready to focus only on each other.

Sample chapters

♥ "Pimpin'" — Dating multiple guys

♥ Multi-dating pros and cons

♥ Your Date-A-Base — tracking multiple suitors

♥ "Hot bunking" your beaus

♥ Are you a "Let's Make a Deal" type of dater?

♥ Assume there are other women

♥ Dating's revolving door

♥ How long do you hedge your bet?

♥ Beware of multi-tasking when multi-dating

♥ Back burner beaus

♥ The boyfriend phone

Moving On Gracefully: Break Up Without Heartache

"Breaking up" sounds so high school, doesn't it? But part of the dating process is saying something when one of you decides not to date the other anymore. Going "poof" is not a mature or respectful option in midlife.

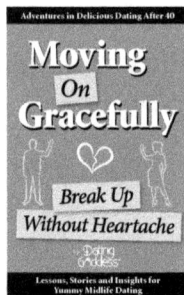

This book focuses on surviving a breakup, whether you initiate it or not. Either way, it's never easy to break up if you have developed any fondness toward the other.

Sample chapters

💚 Hello — goodbye: How to say no thanks after meeting

💚 Releasing back into the dating pool

💚 50 ways to leave your lover? 4 ways not to leave your suitor

💚 Breaking up is hard to do — right

💚 Why men go "poof"

💚 How to trump being dumped

💚 When breaking up is a "Get Out of Jail Free" card

💚 How to detect the end is near

💚 Failed relationships' blessings

💚 He's broken up with you — he just didn't tell you

💚 Rejection is protection

From Fear to Frolic: Get Naked Without Getting Embarrassed

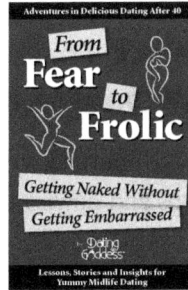

This book focuses on what you need to consider and know before getting physically intimate with a man you're dating. This is nerve-wracking to many midlife women. This book will prepare you.

Sample chapters

💜 Sleepover do's and don'ts

💜 Does he want in your life — or just in your bedroom?

💜 Getting naked with him the first time

💜 An excuse to seduce or how important is bedroom bliss?

💜 What to ask yourself before getting naked with him

💜 Are you and your guy on the same sexual time line?

💜 Sharing your sexual owner's manual with him

💜 What women need from a man before having sex

💜 Why too-soon midlife sex is like non-fat food

💜 How dating sex is like waffles

💜 Too-soon seduction: "I'm special, but not THAT special"

Ironing Out Dating Wrinkles: Work Through Challenges Without Getting Steamed

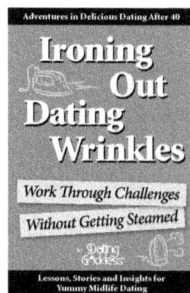

Nearly all relationships have some ups and downs. Part of getting to know someone is knowing how they work through relationship misunderstandings.

This book focuses on how to work through the inevitable hiccups that happen when you are getting to know each other. If you can both deal with challenges, the bond deepens and you find yourself smitten.

Sample chapters

💜 When your guy vexes you, ask what your highest self would do

💜 The first fight

💜 You want boo; he wants boo-ty

💜 Where's the line between getting your needs met and being selfish?

💜 Expressing your upset with your guy

💜 Is his toothbrush in your cabinet too soon?

💜 Do you love how he loves you?

💜 Is he collecting data on how to make you happy?

💜 Be careful of being smitten

💜 Exclusivity: How and when to broach it

www.ingramcontent.com/pod-product-compliance
Lightning Source LLC
Chambersburg PA
CBHW051730020426
42333CB00014B/1238